301 MORE WAYS TO HAVE FUN AT WORK

DAVE HEMSATH

Illustrations by JEEVAN SIVASUBRAMANIAM

D0044109

BK

BERRETT-KOEHLER PUBLISHERS, INC.
San Francisco

Berrett-Koehler Publishers, Inc.
450 Sansome Street, Suite 1200
San Francisco, CA 94111-3320
Tel: (415) 288-0260; Fax: (415) 362-2512
www.bkconnection.com

ORDERING INFORMATION

Quantity sales. Special discounts are available on quantity purchases by corporations, associations, and others. For details, contact the "Special Sales Department" at the Berrett-Koehler address above.

Individual sales. Berrett-Koehler publications are available through most bookstores. They can also be ordered direct from Berrett-Koehler: Tel: (800) 929-2929; Fax: (802) 864-7626; www.bkconnection.com

Orders for college textbook/course adoption use. Please contact Berrett-Koehler: Tel: (800) 929-2929; Fax: (802) 864-7626.

Orders by U.S. trade bookstores and wholesalers. Please contact Publishers Group West, 1700 Fourth Street, Berkeley, CA 94710. Tel: (510) 528-1444; Fax (510) 528-3444.

Printed in the United States of America
Printed on acid-free and recycled paper that is composed of 80% recovered fiber, including 30% post consumer waste.

Library of Congress Cataloging-in-Publication Data
Hemsath, Dave, 1961-
   301 more ways to have fun at work / Dave Hemsath; illustrations by Jeevan Sivasubramaniam.
      p. cm.
   Rev. and expanded ed. of: 301 ways to have fun at work.
   Includes bibliographical references and index.
   ISBN 1-57675-118-X
      1. Personnel management. 2. Work environment. 3. Work—Psychological aspects. I. Title: 301 more ways to have fun at work. II. Hemsath, Dave, 1961- 301 ways to have fun at work. III. Title

HF5549 .H3928 2001
658.3—dc21   2001025038

First Edition
06 05 04 03 02 01   10 9 8 7 6 5 4 3 2 1

This book is dedicated to my family:

To my Mom and Dad,
Bill and Virginia Hemsath
To my wife, Gayle
and
To my boys, Mike, Derek, and Scott

Being well-loved makes me Fun-loving.

TABLE OF CONTENTS

PREFACE

In the years since Leslie Yerkes and I wrote *301 Ways to Have Fun at Work,* it has been my pleasure to continue speaking on having fun at work, hearing others tell about their fun at work, and (most of all!) having my own fun at work. For all these experiences I am truly grateful.

Why write another book on fun at work? Since *301 Ways* was published, dozens of new ideas have been faxed, e-mailed, and handed to me on how others are having fun at work. The encouragement of these individuals and the desire to share the bounty are two major reasons for writing a follow-up. More important, many business areas were not addressed in the first book. Originally, Leslie and I organized the fun into categories that best expressed our already-collected ideas: Communication, Work Environment, Training, Meetings, Recognition, and Teams. For *301 More Ways*, the ideas seemed to self-select into new areas of interest: Hiring and Retention, Corporate Culture, Leadership, Customer Service, Sales and Marketing, and Fun Events.

How fast the world changes! In these few short years, the corporate jungle has morphed from traditional brick-and-mortar businesses to high-flying dot.com companies. With these frenetic changes in the business world has come an almost fanatical interest in quality-of-life issues. These issues are thoroughly interwoven into the new workplace. The business climate is evolving constantly, and the contemporary workforce is highly sought-after, mobile, and—maybe for the first time in history—less concerned with monetary rewards than about how work affects their preferred way of living. The message to both employers and vendors is crystal clear: I'll work for you, or I'll do business with you, only if I am enjoying the experience.

The premise behind *301 Ways* was that fun can be used as a strategic weapon to help companies achieve extraordinary results in training, meetings, team building, and a wide array of other corporate activities. The premise behind *301 More Ways* is that, in the new millennium, it is not enough to help organizations achieve extraordinary results; organizations must use fun as a strategic weapon to help people become extraordinary individuals. New- and old-economy companies have one common denominator: it is the ideas and efforts of individuals that make their organization great.

I would also call your attention to another valuable resource for bringing fun into the workplace—a new book by Leslie Yerkes, who co-authored with me *301 Ways to Have Fun at Work*. Leslie's new book, titled "Fun Works," offers real case studies of companies (such as Pike Place Fish market, Blackboard, Inc.) that have integrated fun into their everyday ways of doing their work. It shows how integrating fun into work helps these companies succeed and pays off in higher productivity, creativity, and employee retention.

301 More Ways is a compilation of great ideas from great individuals. I would like to acknowledge the many individuals who made this book possible. Many of its ideas were gleaned from personal interviews and correspondence (both electronic and snail mail) with fun people who love to share their ideas. Some of the book was the result of research, often achieved through good friends who kept me informed. Several thousand surveys over the past year produced many new ideas and opinions. I am excited and happy to share them with you.

Many thanks to my family and friends, who as always were generous with their support. Thanks to Lauren Ogan, for your contributions and for being a great sounding board. Thanks again to my business partner, Patrick, and my co-workers Lucy, Doug, Jeff, and Charita. It is great to have a workplace that tolerates my unusual work habits—and attire! Thanks to my new and old friends at Berrett-Koehler, especially Kristen, for taking time out of your busy schedule for a little FUN. A special thank you (and I love you) to my wife Gayle, and my growing (in number and in size) boys, Michael, Derek, and Scott. My greatest source of fun is being a part of your lives.

Dave Hemsath
Rocky River, Ohio
January 2001

FUN ONE MORE TIME

INTRODUCTION

Fun at work has become an oxymoron for many successful, motivated workers throughout the world. Work *can* be fun. But, as many people are finding out, when you start any new undertaking with noble intentions and an ambitious goal (like having fun at work), fun can be a lot of, well, *work*. The hardest thing to overcome in having fun at work is inertia. Taking action on anything, let alone a fun initiative, is difficult for most of us because it takes us out of our comfort zone. But, by taking action and making fun a priority in the workplace, many organizations have excelled in areas where challenges and problems had been the norm. People have used fun as a tool to improve business meetings, communicate effectively, and create an environment that works for everyone.

Our original premise for *301 Ways to Have Fun at Work* was that fun may be the single most important trait of highly effective organizations. We received overwhelmingly positive response to the thousands of surveys distributed after that first book was published. Results showed that having fun at work had a significant impact on an employee's creativity, productivity, morale, job satisfaction, and retention. Perhaps having fun at work is not the *one* trait that makes companies succeed, but employing tactics to increase workplace fun may be the most important trait of highly effective employees. More important, employees themselves value fun as a way to become more successful at work. According to a study conducted by Interim Services, nearly 75% of employees surveyed believed that promoting fun and closer workplace relationships would make their jobs more attractive and reduce turnover.

Since publishing *301 Ways* I have continued to explore possible correlations between our most satisfied workers and areas of business life not included in the original book. What fun activities are people using to improve customer service, sales and marketing, human resources? How does fun relate to leadership skills? These questions provided the basis for a new survey, and *301 More Ways* contains the inspiring responses to the survey.

HOW TO USE THIS BOOK

I have written *301 More Ways to Have Fun at Work* as an easy-to-use reference for people who want to enliven their workplace. By no means is this a text meant to be read from beginning to end. Choose an area of interest, find an appropriate idea, and put the book down. It is time to have some fun! Put that new idea into action, then come back for more. Read the book front to back, back to front, or just skip around. I assure you there is no hidden message. (That is, unless you put this book on a turntable and play it backwards. Then you will find out *pssst! Paul is dead.*)

The book is organized into six distinct sections to help you find a fun idea that suits your needs. For those of you who want the rest of the story, there is Fun Focus, a look at a specific company or individual who exemplifies a fun attitude. The sections are:

hires — **Hiring and Retention:** Fun-atics Need Apply

culture — **Corporate Culture:** Fun R Us

leaders — **Leadership:** Fun from the Top Down

service — **Customer Service:** Priority Fun

sales — **Sales & Marketing:** Fun Sells

events — **Events:** Gone Funnin'! Be Back Soon

Also, look for the fun icons throughout the book:

Interesting facts regarding workplace issues.

Fun resources for you to use in your own workplace.

Interesting and fun quotes for you to ponder.

A new area. This icon is used for when something definitely not fun happens in the workplace. These are examples of the dark side of a fun workplace. Beware of the dark side.

This icon will appear when I have a comment on something or when I am retelling a story from my own workplace. I have a twisted sense of humor (see dead Paul earlier). So, if there is a commentary that seems odd or out of place, it is typically a joke (although I might be the only one who gets it).

Throughout the book there are actual examples of things people do at work to have fun. I have tried to eliminate any idea that is in poor taste or that may offend someone. *I want to make fun as inclusive as possible, so we all can have fun together.* One guideline I try to follow before telling a humorous story or joke is this: if you have to look over your shoulder first, then it is inappropriate to be sharing at work. I have tried to follow this guideline while writing this book.

Following the fun ideas is a review of the 12-step method for the fun-impaired workplace. There you will find out what we learned (if anything) after writing *301 Ways to Have Fun at Work*. At the end of the book is a list of suggested readings. I included only books that I know have helped people create lasting fun workplaces.

A common question that is often asked of me is how companies become fun places to work. I address that issue in Dave's Hierarchy of Fun. Please read on.

DAVE'S HIERARCHY
OF FUN

(WITH APOLOGIES TO ABRAHAM MASLOW)

I am asked often how companies can start having fun, or how can my company become more fun. In *301 Ways to Have Fun at Work,* Leslie Yerkes and I introduced a 12-step plan (for the fun-impaired workplace). This plan gave specific steps for anyone to start having fun at work.

I also have been asked, in a much broader sense, "How do organizations have fun?" Now, I don't have any degrees in organizational behavior and I am not a Ph.D. in group psychology. I am just a guy who admires fun people. I make observations and report what other people are doing. But I have drawn some conclusions regarding fun workplaces, and I have compiled them into what I call Dave's Hierarchy of Fun. It follows Abraham Maslow's hierarchy of needs, although I doubt anyone will be teaching Dave's hierarchy in Psych 101. In Maslow's famous theory on human motivation, people move through different levels of satisfaction as their more basic needs are met. Maslow used a pyramid (or at least my teachers did), indicating that everyone starts at the bottom. In this first stage, everyone is motivated by the need for food and shelter. When these needs are met, people may progress by stages to the highest-level needs, which Maslow calls self-actualization, or the fulfillment of one's greatest human potential. Not everyone achieves self-actualization in their lifetime; frequently people get stuck somewhere in the middle.

Because I am a much more inclusive guy than Abe, in Dave's hierarchy it is much easier to reach the pinnacle of a fun organization. Here's how I perceive the progression of needs in a fun company.

IDENTITY

PARTICIPATION

TRUST

COMMUNICATION

ACCEPTANCE AND INCLUSION

ACCEPTANCE AND INCLUSION

The first requirement for allowing fun to happen at work is that people have a feeling of acceptance and inclusion. In general, people are not going to do anything "different" at work until they become comfortable in the workplace. You could say the foundation for a fun workplace is in place once people are comfortable at work. Fun is not fun unless everyone can be included. So, what if someone doesn't want to take part in an activity that everyone else in planning? My answer to this is that everyone must have the *opportunity* to be included. Remember, not all fun activities appeal to everyone. When all co-workers have the opportunity to participate, then you are developing the foundation of acceptance and inclusion.

COMMUNICATION

If the lines of communication are active within an organization, fun can thrive. With poor communication, fun is stifled. I mean communication in its broadest sense. Corporate communication in the form of a mission statement, or company-wide goals, is critical. Policies and procedures, sales objectives, and communication of holidays and company functions are all vitally important to maintaining the comfort level of employees. Newsletters, bulletins, Post-it® notes, announcements over a PA system, and whatever else it takes: fun can grow in an environment where information is shared freely.

Communication on an interdepartmental level or personal level is also key to building a successful fun workplace. Employees should get to know about one another's lives outside the office. This will build a sense of caring and trust between individuals. However, gossip and badmouthing other employees is destructive and should be stopped. Most problems occur when people don't sit down and talk openly with one another. Without positive communication you can't move to the next level.

TRUST

The reason most organizations don't have a productive fun culture is because they never reach the level of trust. Communication is the stumbling block for most organizations; when there is poor communication there is typically very little trust within the organization. I mean trust in management, trust in your co-worker, even trust in your customers. It is a common practice of the worker who feels unappreciated to mock the intelligence or motivations (or whatever) of the leaders of the company. Basically, employees in these situations don't trust. Can you even imagine the average employee of Southwest Airlines questioning whether CEO Herb

Kelleher has their best interest in mind, or whether CEO Scott McNealy is competent to make the best decisions for Sun Microsystems. The thought is ludicrous. Yet both Southwest and Sun Microsystems are benchmarks for fun creative workplaces. Their employees trust them.

Companies often pass down decisions and changes that affect everyone from the highest to the lowest-level worker without ever explaining their rationale. If upper management would trust the intelligence and reasonableness of the people they've hired to give insight into their own thinking, employees would in turn trust that management knows what it is doing.

Employees who have the trust of their own management and co-workers, and in turn trust their management, are free to add some fun to their worklife. Management will trust them to be appropriate and to maintain productivity. People can then trust their own instincts and allow themselves to be spontaneous and to have fun.

PARTICIPATION

Once a trusting relationship has developed, the next level for an enlightened workplace is to get everyone involved. Make fun inclusive. The infectiousness of fun can spread fast, but only if everyone is given a chance to participate. On a company's road toward the pinnacle of fun, this is where you gain an unstoppable momentum. Invite new departments, your suppliers, or even your customers to participate in your fun activities. This is where you can vertically integrate fun into all aspects of the business. Can you imagine the energy, creativity, problem-solving ability, and productivity that could be developed by several organizations working together in a climate of cooperation and fun?

A common obstacle to participation is the separation of departments, offices, and individuals from each other or from the company headquarters. How do we get everyone to participate? I want to answer this question by using an analogy based on the book *Orbiting the Giant Hairball*, by Gordon MacKenzie (OpusPocus Publishing, 1996). In his book, Gordon relates his experiences working for Hallmark Cards. The hairball in his book is the tangled mess of a large bureaucratic organization. His philosophy is that, in order to survive and thrive in corporate life, an individual must connect and interact with the hairball but do so without getting trapped. When trying to increase participation in fun activities in a corporate setting, you have to communicate, invite, and include as many offices or departments as possible without getting caught in the hairball. Is it easy? No, but it is vital for the continued success of any fun initiative. The benefits to your company are limitless.

IDENTITY

An organization that has climbed the pyramid of Dave's Hierarchy of Fun reaches the level of enlightened fun when they begin to make the fun special to themselves. You know you have reached this level when people outside of your company know you for your fun activities. It is not necessary to be known to the general public, but within your geographic region or within your industry. For example: Manco, a manufacturer of duct tape, is known for its Annual Duck Challenge, a festival celebrating corporate successes, capped off by the CEO swimming in the company duck pond. Southwest Airlines is known for many off-the-wall antics in the airline industry. Even individuals can reach the pinnacle of enlightened fun when they become known for the way they bring fun to everything they do. And it doesn't have to be in a corporate setting. People like Bill Parschen, a principal at an elementary school in suburban Ohio, is known for administering a great school but also for being a leader in making learning fun.

Anyone can reach the top of the fun world. It is a process, just like any other aspect of your worklife. Just remember to start with yourself, get others involved, and use some of the ideas in this book to get it all going.

HIRING AND RETENTION

FUN-ATICS **NEED APPLY**

HIRING AND RETENTION

FUN-ATICS
NEED APPLY

Possibly the biggest change over the last several years has been the | hiring | policy, the philosophy that underlies attracting, hiring, and retaining employees in your organization. In what many people consider the "good old days," there was an abundance of qualified and | talented | individuals who would love to work for your company. Not only would they work for you but they would also be grateful, loyal, and committed to the goals of the organization. All the company would have to do for these | employees | was to ensure that they got paid regularly and (eventually) received some vacation time. These old-style employees were easy to motivate. It was work or get fired.

Welcome to the new millenium. It **is** the age of low unemployment. Hiring, training, and firing have become time-consuming and expensive. How do successful organizations find and attract quality individuals to their company? It's not just pay. It's not just benefits. Many successful companies are finding that the **best** way to attract, hire, and retain the most creative and productive employees is to have fun with them. Although some people may want to make fun *of* the new rookies, **when** you are having fun *with* them, you'll find that hiring and retaining the best candidates is a breeze.

By making **fun** an integral part of your recruiting, I think you'll be surprised at how painless finding and keeping top candidates can be. Dull people need not apply, we're looking for fun-atics!

T hinking on your feet is a must when interviewing, but never before have job applicants had to think and act like they do now. At a recent interview at Zefer, an Internet consulting firm in Boston, a job applicant was asked to build something with a box of LEGOs and given only five minutes to finish his creation. The clever interviewee came up with an aerated cognac snifter and was awarded a job offer. The fast-paced world of high technology has led to interesting techniques that help test a candidate's ability to collaborate and think under pressure. Brain teasers, riddles, and group games are common ways to evaluate new talent.

▼　▼　▼

W hen Gary Quick, CEO of Quick Solutions Inc. of Columbus, Ohio, founded his company back in 1991, he felt that his biggest potential problem would be hiring and keeping good workers. Quick starts out fast by making a great first impression with new employees. "Sometime during that first week, we send a basket of pasta products to the home. It's amazing how that boosts the morale, not just of that person, but of his or her spouse," says Gary. After staying with the company for 36 months, employees become eligible for the special benefits program. Its two major features are free monthly house-cleaning and a $1200 annual voucher for personal travel.

▼   ▼   ▼

There are very few people at Cisco who don't have the opportunity to leave for a 50% pay raise any time they want. What keeps them here is that it's fun, it's exciting, and you can make a difference.
John Chambers, CEO, Cisco Systems

hires

Instead of trying to paint the perfect picture of your job opening when placing an ad, maybe you should try what Premier Courier Inc. of Columbus, Ohio, does. They definitely don't have rose-tinted glasses. The ad reads: "We're interested in hiring a semi-obnoxious, pushy account representative for the very boring repetitious job of selling our business services." Sounds great so far. "Applicants should have a skin like an alligator and the desire to suffer their way to earn what they're worth under our combination salary and commission compensation program."

According to Ron Dillard of Premier Courier: "It's basic Marketing 101. The tighter the labor market, the more creative you've got to be." The ads have been successful. In the past, Ron might have gotten only about five responses, but 50 people responded to this ad. Having fun in hiring helps Ron have fun at work. "You have to read it tongue-in-cheek. We've got a good crew of people who care about the company."

Cleveland Plain Dealer,
"Humor baits hook in employer's want ad."
(11/7/00)

> **Companies have to go at their own pace and develop their own style of fun. You can't just dump a bag of tricks and say "You WILL have fun!" It won't work.**   **Matt Weinstein,** *Managing to Have Fun* **(quoted in the** *San Francisco Examiner***)**

▼   ▼   ▼

Work Hard, Play Hard. This is the most used (or *over*used) slogan in the new world of attracting employees. It is what follows that often belies the words. In a recent full-page employment advertisement, Hyland Software not only fulfills the promise of a fun place to work but also promotes serious aspects of the company and sets forth the qualities of the individuals they want to hire. The text of the ad reads: "Building a great software company has taken a lot of hard work by some talented people. And, to put it simply, we're having a blast. Sure, the casual dress, the pinball machines, and the noontime kickball games make this a fun place to spend the day (and the occasional night). But the

hires

real thrill comes from delivering products and services that delight our customers and frustrate our competitors." Their list of benefits is well worth reading: "Great Pay, Stock Options, Take Your Boat or Jet Ski to Work (Summer Only), Training Incentive Plan, Free Candy, Paid Overtime, Kickball Lunch, Life Insurance, Cool T-Shirts, Sombrero Wearing Classes, Hospitalization, Occasional Free Lunches, Disability Insurance, Paid Vacations, Free Pen and Paper (Stapler in Your Second Year), 401(k) Plan, Free Llama for Every New Employee, Casual Attire, Sick Leave, More Free Lunches, Profit Sharing." The ad for Hyland Software is very cleverly put together. Even the fine print is humorous: "The llamas are void in the states of MI, KE, LA, AL, ST, OP, RE, AD, IN, GT, HI, S."

▼   ▼   ▼

Because of the increased competition for quality employees, recruiters have crossed the line between aggressive and obsessive. According to *Trend Alert* **(August 23, 2000), some of the most aggressive recruiters are actually operating like**

fun

bounty hunters, following prospects into parking garages and hiring salespeople right off competitors' sales floors. An extreme example is that of recruiters calling competing hospitals and offering anyone who answers the phone a 20% raise to change jobs. Aggressive un-fun techniques like these are not the way to build a long-term devoted staff.

▼   ▼   ▼

Accounting firms are not typically known for their sense of humor and fun, but Keister Radice and Company, a Rocky River, Ohio–based accounting firm, finds that the quality of applicants improves dramatically when they spice up their help-wanted ads with fun. A recent job ad for an accounting position included job specifics and the header BEAN COUNTERS NEED NOT APPLY. Managing partner Steve Furrer feels that unorthodox ads attract the type of out-of-the-box thinkers they are trying to find.

hires

Caliper, a psychological testing and human resources consulting firm in Princeton, New Jersey, surveyed more than 180 executives and discovered that nearly 40% of departing employees felt they were ill-matched with their jobs. Unfortunately, the tight job market has caused many employers to fill positions with anyone who is remotely appropriate and, according to Caliper president Herbert Greenburg, "These short-term solutions rarely work." The survey revealed some interesting reasons people quit. Twenty-six percent found higher paying jobs, 18% left for personal reasons, and 11% left because of co-worker conflict. Quirky responses included "There was a demon residing in our computer network," "My pet bird is ill and I have to take care of him," and "I'm going to the bathroom" (he never returned).

▼　▼　▼

First-rate people hire first-rate people. Second-rate people hire third-rate people.　　Leo Rosten

fun

Most employers look for the job candidate who has related job experience and the type of personality that would fit into the company culture. Not so, says Morris Shechtman, a Chicago-based employee retention and development strategist. *Continental* magazine (September 1999) quotes Schechtman advising: "Hire employees who introduce healthy conflict and divergent views that can spur real growth . . . look for high risk people." Schechtman feels that "in today's unpredictable business environment, companies need people who can roll with the changes that occur frequently." A spontaneous, fun-loving job candidate is the type of person who can create the positive turmoil to keep a company competitive.

▼ ▼ ▼

Forrester Research, a high-tech research firm in Cambridge, Massachusetts, estimates that U.S. employers spent $105 million on online employment ads in 1998, and they expect spending to increase to $1.7 billion by 2003.

hires

$\mathbb{A}$ ccording to the January 10, 2000, issue of *Fortune* magazine, here are the top 10 companies to work for and why they are great companies:

1. **Container Store, Dallas**
   After 10 years, employees are allowed to take sabbaticals.

2. **Southwest Airlines, Dallas**
   Southwest is famous for its wacky culture.

3. **Cisco Systems, San Jose**
   Offers on-the-spot bonuses of up to $2000 for exceptional performance.

4. **TD Industries, Dallas**
   Workers get 2 weeks of paid personal time off after 1 year, in addition to vacations.

5. **Synovus Financial, Columbus, Georgia**
   Provides pension and bonuses of up to 21% of gross pay, plus stock options.

6. **SAS Institute, Cary, North Carolina**
   Has onsite child care, health center with physicians and dentists, massage therapist, wooded campus, and profit sharing.

7. **Edward Jones, St. Louis**
   Brokers qualify for twice-a-year, expense-

fun

paid jaunts for two to places like Alaska and Pebble Beach.

8. Charles Schwab, San Francisco
Massages during busy periods.

9. Goldman Sachs, New York
Employees working late are ferried home by a free limo service.

10. MBNA, Wilmington, Delaware
Six child-care centers, and college scholarships of up to $32,000 for employees' kids.

▼   ▼   ▼

*S*tephanie Armour, of *USA Today,* concurs that many employers are taking innovative approaches to recruiting in a tight job market. George Bailey, with the consulting firm of Watson Wyatt Worldwide in Bethesda, Maryland, states: "It's a major trend in the workplace. Companies are finding what they're really competing for isn't just market and customers. It's employees." Some companies that have taken to fun recruiting:

hires

- Sprint Business Creative Marketing Center in Dallas, Texas, throws ice-cream socials and karaoke contests for employees. Rubber pig noses, juggling balls, and other toys sit in conference rooms to foster brainstorming and creativity. Margie Tippen, of Sprint, says "It has absolutely helped in our recruiting, as well as in the retention of our employees."

- CEO Dave Duffield, of Peoplesoft in Pleasanton, California, does comedy routines at quarterly meetings and has employees join his "Raving Dave's" rock band. Kit Robinson, also from Peoplesoft, says "We have a low turnover rate—it's a fun place to work."

- At Cognex, a software manufacturer in Natick, Massachusetts, employees are encouraged to play ultimate Frisbee on company grounds, visit the onsite pinball room, enjoy a Friday afternoon social, or take advantage of free movie nights. Because there is a lot of competition for the best employees in the Boston area, Cognex encourages prospective candidates to use the World Wide Web to learn more about recruiting packages and to promote their unique culture.

fun

A survey of 5500 new college grads said that "enjoying what I do" was most important to them in a job. Next came "opportunities to use skills/abilities," followed by "opportunity for personal development." Benefits ranked fifth, and "lots of money" was in ninth place, in the study of National Association of Colleges and Employers.

Personnel Journal

▼   ▼   ▼

As the labor market tightens, recruiters are trying a lot of crazy things to track down the perfect candidate. According to Roger Herman, of the Herman Group Weekly Trend Alert (alert@herman.net), corporate recruiters are now spending their time at spring break hot spots such as Daytona Beach, and have even been found spending time on ski slopes in an attempt to hook up with qualified candidates. Now some branches of Manpower, Inc., are getting local churches involved. Herman states "It's an interesting win-win approach. As part of their effort to fill job orders, Manpower encourages

hires

branches to pay churches $50 to $75 for each candidate referral." After spending spring break at Daytona Beach, many recruiters probably find it necessary to spend at little extra time at church!

▼   ▼   ▼

According to *USA Today*, people now change jobs an average of nine times before they are 32 years old. This averages out to 1 year, 4 months on the job. I guess we need to give people a better reason to stay.

▼   ▼   ▼

Humor and fun have become a competitive advantage to companies that are hiring. Some of the most talented and capable people are actually self-selecting themselves into fun corporate cultures. The founders of Remedy Corp., a software company in Mountain View,

fun

California, actually identified fun as a key value of the new company back in 1990. The company has grown, doubling its size and revenue for more than five consecutive years, while keeping a focus on the fun. According to Gillian Flynn, of the *San Francisco Examiner*: "Applicants may find themselves being interviewed at a mini-car race. New hires have padded up to sumo-wrestle their bosses. The Remedy parking lot has featured obstacle courses and human foosball games in which soccer players are linked to each other by poles."

The good times have paid off on the bottom line for Remedy. Their cost per hire is about $6100 compared to industry costs of $8450. Remedy also retains its best employees longer—two years longer than industry averages. Much of the success is attributed to executives' continued belief that good times lead to good business.

Richard Wilson was manager of a high-stress business for a company in Northern California. During his exit interview he was informed that he was being terminated because his employees had repeatedly been caught laughing too much. So much for the power of laughter in that workplace.

▼   ▼   ▼

S alaries and benefits are not the main motivations behind today's workforce. Many companies are finding that to keep their best people takes more than just dollars and cents. Jack Schacht, CEO of Illinois Trade Association, says "Our employees don't work just for economic benefits. If people feel they can express themselves, it gives them a sense of meaning." Schacht knows what he is talking about; over the last five years his company has experienced zero turnover. Schacht tries to find out where employee interests lie and makes an effort to incorporate those interests into the work environment. One worker helped establish a local youth center and was asked to coordinate a volunteer program for the United Way, all on company time. For the less ambitious, Illinois Trade has arranged monthly massages for any employee who wants one. Employees interested in nontraditional health care can seek treatment through chiropractic, herbal therapy, and other alternative forms, all at the expense of Illinois Trade. It appears that this policy would be a tremendous expense to the company, but Schacht says "It's very important that we keep turnover to a minimum because we put so much into training our employees."

Fortune

One of the reasons I've stayed here is because of the relaxed atmosphere. Once you get all the frustrations out, you're ready to work.

Raymond Tyson,
after winning a game of Ping Pong,
on why he enjoys working at EMJ America

hires

▼ ▼ ▼

DAVE'S TOP TEN LIST

FUN FOODS FOR WORK

1. Pizza
2. Wings
3. Popcorn
4. Ice Cream / Sundaes
5. Donuts
6. Hot Dogs
7. Beer
8. Twizlers (they make mouths happy)
9. Cookies
10. Tacos / Mini Tacos

▼ ▼ ▼

C heri Gudaitis, manager of the accounting support division of ELINVAR, a North Carolina–based recruiting and consulting firm, believes the success her company has achieved is based partly on their ability to have fun with their clients and candidates. Cheri suggests these steps to using fun in hiring:

▼ Due to the stressful nature of hiring, you need to be creative and incorporate excitement and fun into the interview process. Creating a relaxed environment promotes an open forum, which can enhance a positive experience for everyone and create a strong rapport between the interviewer and the candidate.

▼ First impressions mean everything, therefore always greet your candidates with a warm, welcoming smile. Encourage each candidate to share funny and memorable stories and be sure to reciprocate. Laughter is healthy and contagious, and it strengthens the working relationship.

▼ Celebration is the most enjoyable part of the hiring process. Do not forget to congratulate your candidates with a gift. I always send a gift certificate to their favorite restaurant, sporting event, or store, and it always brings a smile to their face.

hires

A study by Interim Services showed nearly 75% of employees feel promoting fun and closer workplace relationships would make jobs more attractive and reduce turnover. *USA Today*

▼   ▼   ▼

W ho said it's not fun to go to school? According to *Fortune* magazine, several companies, including Hewlett-Packard and Barnett Banks, have sponsored public schools at their worksites. American Bankers Insurance Group in Miami has gone as far as spending $2.4 million to build a satellite school right on its corporate campus. There is no skipping classes here! Parents are encouraged to visit their children at lunchtime and after school.

Phillip Sharkey, head of the human resource department, says "The school helps recruit and retain good employees." By reducing the turnover rate from 13% on average to 5% for employees with children in the school, American Bankers should recoup its investment in just over 10 years.

fun

large pay raise might sound like a great incentive to a prospective employee, but it actually might be a detriment to hiring the most qualified individual.

It sounds funny, but the IRS makes it more advantageous for employees to be compensated in nontraditional methods. Instead of a $5000 a year raise (100% taxed), provide $5000 a year in daycare services or $5000 a year in onsite gym time or $5000 in educational opportunities, all 100% nontaxable. With a little creativity, nontaxable corporate benefits can make the difference when hiring and keeping the most talented people.

▼   ▼   ▼

Break the Ice: 200 Fun Questions to Help Break the Ice at Business Meetings, Training Sessions and Other Gatherings, **by Scott Saalman. Published by Cornerstone Publishing, Virginia Beach, Virginia. ($7.95)**

hires

D allas-based Southwest Airlines, known for its quirky culture, sometimes treats job candidates to a theme day. Interviewers dress in pajamas or beach wear, while candidates pick from props such as sunglasses. "We try to make it fun from beginning to end," says Sherry Phelps at Southwest. "We try to capitalize on that environment to attract employees." *USA Today*

▼   ▼   ▼

I never did a day's work in my life; it was all fun.

Thomas Edison

▼   ▼   ▼

E ven when you do everything right, some employees leave—sometimes due to a transfer or promotion, sometimes for health reasons, and sometimes it is just time for a change. If you have had fun hiring and retaining your employees, what's to say you can't have fun

fun

saying goodbye. A San Francisco company did just that. They covered the elevator with paper and "Velcro-ed" markers to the walls. In large letters they wrote "Good Luck Mike, We'll Miss You." Everyone who rode the elevator that day could pen their own message, and some people even added photographs. I am sure Mike took with him fond memories of the affection of his co-workers.

A side benefit to a pleasant departure is that, when employees leave with a warm feeling about the experience of working there, they will be more likely to recommend that job-seeking peers check out their former company.

▼ ▼ ▼

All work and no play makes Jack a dull boy.
Stephen King, *The Shining*

hires

HYLAND SOFTWARE, WORK HARD, PLAY HARD. (NO, REALLY!)

On a recent trip to New York City, I had the pleasure of sitting in the midst of several people, all of whom were wearing OnBase shirts. They obviously worked together and enjoyed each other's company. Being a big baseball fan, I had to know what was up (Whaaaasup?) with OnBase. What I found was a dynamic high-tech company that has a recruiting department with a totally off-the-wall sense of humor.

Hyland Software is a developer and marketer of a software application called OnBase. Their software enables companies to operate more efficiently by storing, retrieving, and routing their documents online. Hyland's success has made them one of the fastest-growing companies in the United States. The company motto is, you guessed it, "Work Hard, Play Hard." (Yawn!) When I heard this, I told my traveling companion that it was nice talking to him, but it was time to catch up on my sleep. As someone who writes about fun at work, I can't tell you how many times I have heard about companies that "work hard and play hard" and allow casual dress on the third Friday of every month. Usually the companies that claim to work hard and play hard, do neither.

THE DALAI LLAMAS OF FUN

Even though Hyland has a well-worn company motto, they must be doing something right. Their

fun

CORPORATE CULTURE

FUN R US

Corporate culture is one of those indefinable terms about which everyone seems to have their own idea. Marvin Bower, author of *The Will to Manage* (McGraw-Hill, 1966), describes the informal cultural elements of a business as "the way we do things around here." The ways people do things around their workplace can affect virtually every aspect of their business: who gets promoted, what is appropriate attire, where people eat, even who they work and socialize with. In my view, culture is not only about how we do things but also about why we do things. Culture affects our corporate belief system and values.

There are many companies who put a value on creating a fun-inspiring workplace. But what

employee turnover rate is an astonishing 3%. Unlike many technology companies who rely on the Internet for recruiting new personnel, they use full-page, four-color newspaper advertising in Sunday papers. The ad's headline is (no, really!) "Work Hard, Play Hard." Interspersed with traditional job descriptions are a variety of photos of employees having fun at work. Excellent salaries are enhanced by traditional incentives, but among the full listing of benefits, candidates will also find some zany incentives like "Free Llama for Every New Employee."

According to Bill Premier, vice president of marketing, "When we used online resources for job recruiting, we were unable to convey our personality. The resumes we received online were also very straightforward. Using the newspaper helps to communicate our story and to attract candidates who will

best fit into our corporate culture. Our screening process is rigorous, with interviews by panels made up of individuals representing various areas of the company. During the first round, candidates are asked to bring Show and Tell (about themselves or their dream job). Some Show and Tell from candidates who were hired included: a hand-crafted cross-stitched pillow depicting various aspects of the person's life; a stuffed Tigger doll symbolizing the interviewee's energetic and upbeat attitude; a neon-pink mask and snorkel worn to demonstrate a sense of humor, self-deprecating nature, and sense of adventure; and a guitar that accompanied the candidate's singing of James Taylor's *Sweet Baby James*.

A HOME RUN FOR FUN

At Hyland, holidays like St. Patrick's Day and Christmas

hires

are company-wide celebrations, usually held at major hotels. Summer is the season for outings at one of the largest amusement parks in the country. Annual meetings have been held at ski resorts. Kickball lunches and barbecues, pool, video games, and foosball, along with company team participation in golf and bowling leagues, help foster togetherness, while periodic, spontaneous e-mail "blasts" invite employees to lunches at special restaurants. Dirt bikes, an RV, and a condominium in Florida are available to all employees on a first-come, first-served basis, but only if they are used for a 7-day period.

It seems as if their philosophy of working hard and playing very hard has been exceedingly successful. Their product is OnBase and so is their culture.

CORPORATE CULTURE

FUN R US

about the companies who don't tag fun as a corporate value.

I believe that corporate personality is not only a reflection of leadership but also **a** mosaic created by individuals who make their own contribution to creating the culture of their workplace. Creating a culture of fun with an eye on productivity, sales goals, and earnings is not hard. Communication and trust allow organizations to excel, both in things business-related and in things **fun** -related. As individuals, we can have the biggest influence on the creation of a fun **culture** . Communication and trust starts with two people and can spread until it infects the entire organization. Fun really is contagious!

Skip your immunization shot this year. Start today to infect your company with fun. Remember: You R Fun!

T hird Federal Savings & Loan in Cleveland, Ohio, was recently ranked by *Fortune* magazine as one of the 100 best companies to work for. If everyone at Third Federal has a sense of humor like that of Marty Kastelic, the manager of the training department, I can see why. For example, Marty relates this story: "On July 28, a pretty severe storm passed through the Cleveland area. Our main office and operations center were without power for most of the following day. Many of the customer-service reps set up shop in the training department, and here are a few things I did to keep things running smoothly:

▼ Because we were short on phone lines at the start of the day, I copied a phone dial and taped it to a zucchini that one of my trainers had brought in. That zucchini cell phone really came in handy! And, if we ran short on food, we could have eaten the phone.

▼ I put on my big plastic ears and told everyone that, because there were so many associates here, we were leaving the outer doors open for circulation. I told them, however, to alert us if they saw any strange people in the area.

▼ To make sure everyone understood the seriousness of our situation, I walked around with a sandwich board that said "Repent, the End Is Near."

Marty is the head of a committee called the "Cabinet of Fun" that meets regularly to inspire fun in the workplace.

▼   ▼   ▼

O ne of the foundations of creating a fun workplace is including everyone in the fun. I am often asked how to do this when the company is decentralized over many cities, countries, and time zones. Amy Jones has come up with one way. Amy works for the automotive systems group of Johnson Controls Inc. A few years ago, to reward and recognize employees for their continuous improvement efforts, Amy and the rest of her group started a program called the Team Rally. Here is how it works. Each of the 250 facilities around the world sends one continuous improvement team to a regional rally, which is held in a nice hotel in a fun city. At the

culture

rallies, the teams present their project in a 15-minute skit. Past teams have been very creative by making a relatively dull subject fun and exciting. There have been skits based on *The Sound of Music*, hosted game shows, and reenactments of popular movies and television shows. Between the skits, they keep things fun with bubble-gum blowing contests, milkshake drinking contests, hula hoop marathons, and toilet paper mummy fashion shows. At each regional event, a panel of judges selects a team to attend the final competition, which is held at Disney World. "We have found that the Team Rally program has become one of our most effective morale tools," says Amy Jones. "The company pride displayed at these events is immeasurable."

The only dress code is that you must.

Scott McNealy, CEO of Sun Microsystems

fun

After five hundred years, William Shakespeare is still in. The popularity of the bard's plays on the big screen is a testament to his lasting words and wit. But the average person is rarely exposed to the writings of Shakespeare. A Raleigh, North Carolina, law firm has taken a cue from the popularity of Shakespeare festivals by creating their own fun festival. Wade Smith, a criminal defense lawyer for Tharrington Smith, came up with the idea for the office to form reading groups for Shakespeare's plays. All employees receive a copy of a play and are given about a month to read it.

They started out with *The Merchant of Venice* and *Hamlet*. Unlike many office reading groups, Smith tries to make the discussion group as meaningful as possible. He has brought in a Shakespearean scholar from Chapel Hill to lead the lecture and to read from the plays. "We work hard to make this a place people look forward to in the morning. If you enjoy work, you are healthy, you live longer, you are kinder to your family. From happy work, great things flow," says Smith.

culture

I have found that a key ingredient to a fun workplace is a high level of communication throughout the organization. At Kimball International in Jasper, Indiana, they have created a fictional corporate spy named Philo Sophy, to report the goings-on at Kimball via letters back to his boss, "Mr. X." The company has created an entire booklet called "The Not-So-Secret Letters of Philo Sophy, Corporate Spy." The Philo campaign also resulted in Wanted posters placed at all their facilities to increase awareness about the book and to build on the cultural themes Philo was reporting. Here is what Philo reported to Mr. X regarding the sense of humor at Kimball.

Dear X:
Seweeeeeeeee!!!!!
One Kimball business unit recently held a hog calling contest. Employees competed with one another to see who would be the best hog caller. Pretty funny stuff.
I mention this because Kimball truly

believes in having a good time and maintaining a sense of humor.

As you may recall, humor is brought up in both the Customer and People sections of Kimball's Guiding Principles:

"We seek to consistently demonstrate a sense of warmth, humor, and mutual respect in our relationships with our customers...

"Kimball has been built upon the tradition of a sense of family and good humor..."

Humor seems to be a daily part of my co-workers' lives. (Okay, so the whoopee cushion on my manager's chair was going a bit too far.) Even leaders and coaches are encouraged to make meetings and training sessions more fun.

Kimball also traditionally has used the Soundboard as a vehicle to relay humor to employees corporate wide.

Let's face it, there aren't many organizations like Kimball out there that can poke fun at themselves every now and then and still get important messages across.

That's all for now. I need to tiptoe over to Pat's office to see what everybody is laughing about. I think I heard the whoopee cushion.

> Da King of Comedy,
> Philo Sophy

culture

Philo's booklet covers a wide range of corporate philosophies, from dealing with customers to creative problem solving, but it also covers the important ground of Eggo-grams and children's Christmas parties. Of course, after spending so much time spying on Kimball, at the end of the booklet Philo turns in his decoder ring and becomes an ex-corporate spy and member of the Kimball team.

▼　　▼　　▼

Sherry Blanchard, of the Burlington Medical Center in Burlington, Iowa, likes to keep their organization buzzing. Sherry and a co-worker decided to sweeten the celebration of National Humor Month by dressing up as bumblebees. Sherry thought that passing out pieces of Bit-O-Honey candies might take the sting out of work and reduce some of the everyday stress of working at a hospital. Cards were taped to each piece of candy with the message "Your smiles are as sweet as a Bit-O-Honey," and "You're a Bit-O-Honey to us!"

fun

Trust is becoming more important as organizations struggle to gain advantage in highly competitive markets. In particular, trust is an absolute necessity when organizations depend on "coordinated empowerment, which gives people the autonomy they need to perform yet requires that they actively collaborate to realize company objectives."
Robert Bruce Shaw, *Trust in the Balance*
(Jossey-Bass, 1997)

Dave's Interprtation: *Not only are trust, empowered employees, and cooperation essential ingredients in any successful organization but, in my experience, they are also the key ingredients to a successful and fun organization.*

▼ ▼ ▼

oel Goodman, founder of The Humor Project Inc., in Sarasota Springs, New York, and author of the book *Laffirmations: 1,001 Ways to Add Humor to Your Life and Work* (Health Communications, 1997), offers some simple steps to creating a more fun workplace:

culture

▼ Develop your comic vision. Look for and find the humor that's all around you.

▼ Ask yourself "How would my favorite comedian portray this situation?"

▼ Adopt a child*like* (not child*ish*) perspective. Kids laugh about 400 times a day, while adults average only 15 laughs a day.

▼ Put humor into your environment. Surround yourself with stimuli such as cartoons and funny quotes. Make humor more accessible to your brain and your tongue.

Reprinted in *Sales & Marketing Magazine*
(March 1999)

▼　▼　▼

The reason most families go to a Disney theme park or other Disney attraction is to have a fun and exciting experience. Disney has consistently been able to offer this experience to millions of visitors around the world because of the culture that is the foundation of the Disney experience. In *Customer Service Management* magazine (September/October 1999), Tony Mosely cites the formula for successful management at Disney. The formula, nicknamed "Pixie Dust," has three elements: (1) training, (2) communication, and (3) care. Together they create pride, which they consider their greatest motivator. Disney's extensive training of "cast members" includes a reminder card that spells out the attitudes Disney expects of its employees. Some of the points include: "Make eye contact and smile," "Greet and welcome each and every guest," "Preserve the magical guest experience," and "Thank each and every guest." It sounds as if the Disney culture is based on the Golden Rule.

▼   ▼   ▼

Try to add a little online fun to your workplace. Visit www.uproar.com or www.amused.com for additional ideas for creating a fun work culture.

culture

H al Harris, of Grundfos Pump Corporation in Fresno, California, related how he has modified an idea that many companies have used. The original game involves having your co-workers bring baby pictures of themselves to the office and post them in a spot that everyone can see. The object is to have everyone try to match their baby face with their current face. With a subtle twist, Hal suggests having everyone bring a picture of their pet to the office and try to match pet owners with their pets. It has been said that pet owners begin to look like their pets over time. What a great activity! See if it's true.

▼　　▼　　▼

S taying fit and healthy is essential to living a long life and, as many businesses are finding out, it is fundamental to leading a productive career. Many organizations are now participating in the annual Dump Your Plump contest as a fun way to encourage employees to take a healthy approach to living. According to Don Alsbro of Benton Harbor, Michigan, the founder of the

Dump Your Plump contest, 96% of the 100,000 participants who have completed the 10-week contest have lost an average of 7.1 pounds per contestant.

Parma Hospital, in Parma, Ohio, enrolled approximately 329 of its 1600 employees as part of the hospital's overall wellness program. "It is important for the public, patients, and family members to perceive hospital employees as being healthy and health conscious," says Pat Moore, chairman of the wellness program. If the corporate culture supports a healthy lifestyle, it tends to be much easier to succeed in losing weight. Steve Musgrave, of the Wellness Council, says "It's so easy to let yourself down, [but it's] more difficult to let the team down." The Dump Your Plump contest web site is www.dumpyour plump.com.

▼   ▼   ▼

For Secretaries' Day, the Outdoor Recreation Center organized events such as the Rat Race Steeplechase or Admin Antics. These featured administrative staff moving through

culture

various departments and competing in cleverly designed events. Events included:

▼ The Disk Drive—teeing up a floppy disk like a golf ball and hitting it with a driver for distance.

▼ Human Bowling—where people on skateboards are the bowling ball and open bottles of water are the pins.

▼ Toss Your Boss—where you dress a blow-up doll like a boss, and toss it for distance.

▼ Telephone Dash—where contestants rush to answer a phone, jumping over and around obstacles while carrying a mock cup of coffee. Winners are determined by the amount of coffee left in the cup.

▼　▼　▼

Carmilla Henry, of First USA bank in Wilmington, Delaware, likes to make everyone feel more relaxed when they come to her office. She leaves a copy of a book called

Business Babble on her desk and encourages visitors to read it. She finds that taking a few minutes to laugh about the absurdity of business-speak helps people become more comfortable with her and is an excellent way to break the ice before a business meeting.

▼   ▼   ▼

The culture surrounding high-tech companies tends to be much less corporate and more Sixties Revival. In the magazine *Fast Company*, writer Katherine Mieszkowski describes a midsummer benefit for the Electric Frontier Foundation. Katherine writes "For one trippy night in San Francisco, venture capitalists and info-babes, software programmers and web-preneurs made their rock 'n' roll dreams come true. For one shining moment, ordinary businesspeople turned into top-of-the-charts rock stars." The night's performances included the Raving Dave's, a band that is a "loose

culture

amalgam of PeopleSoft staffers." According to Mieszkowski, the group started playing together in the office between midnight and 3 a.m. "When CEO Dave Duffield heard the racket, he kicked in $15,000 for equipment—and, in true rock spirit, they named the band after him."

Other acts included: *The Flying Brothers*, named for a venture capitalist at Integral and his brother, an investment banker at First Albany Bank of Boston; *Rockhoppers*, a group made up of stock traders; and blues singer Bryan Simmons of Lotus with guitar-playing Frank Ingari, CEO of Boston-based Shiva, who played with the group *Look & Feel*. "Some industries play golf together," says Allen Razdow, president and CEO of Torrent Systems. "We have jam sessions."

▼　　▼　　▼

There's something about the culture of Vantage One Communications Group that makes it special. It could be the bright purple lobby of their headquarters. Possibly it is the Little Tykes Cozy Coupe, the pedal-powered plastic kids' car that resides in the conference room. Or it could be the creative department, which has recently been remodeled into one big rec room, complete with beanbag chairs and high-speed Internet connectivity. Whatever it is, Dan Rose and Tim Mueller, of the Cleveland-based company, have hit on the formula for success. Ernst & Young awarded them Entrepreneurs of the Year kudos, and they have also made the grade at Case Western Reserve University, where the Weatherhead School of Management included Vantage on their list of outstanding growth companies.

Rose points out that the key to success is keeping the best people: "A pleasant place of employment is often as important as a big paycheck in today's job market. The more enjoyable way to attract and keep employees is to create a culture that is so pleasing, so inviting, so endearing, that people want to come to work." Vantage One's employees are vital to Dan and Tim's achievements and are constantly encouraged to make their mark on the success of the company. Behind the foosball table in the lunchroom, the walls are covered with their handprints. (Source: *Cleveland Style*)

culture

For a bottom-line look at how we're talking 24/7, check out *Business Babble: A Cynic's Dictionary of Corporate Jargon* **by David Olive (Wiley, New York, $14.95). I have just about enough bandwidth left in my brain to read this book.**

▼   ▼   ▼

In our transient society, many companies are throwing people together from all over the world, expecting them to work and be productive together. In the brief and generally intense time we spend at work, it is difficult for individuals to know anything about their co-workers. In a clever use of a popular trivia game, Michelle Ackley, of Aitkin, Minnesota, has newcomers come together and write answers to some questions about their background, where they are from, and any other interesting information they want to share. Questions and answers are read aloud so everyone can learn about their co-workers. She found that many close bonds can be formed by the sharing of amusing anecdotes and information about co-workers and their families.

▼   ▼   ▼

It is time for a second mortgage. It looks like the next beanbag-filled anti-stress room might be at home. According to *Continental* **magazine, "After years of speculation and hype, it looks as though telecommuting—working full- or part-time from a computer at home—and flextime have arrived in the corporate mainstream. A study of 519 American companies with more than 500 employees, conducted by Watson Wyatt Worldwide, a leading global management and human resources consulting firm, found that 51% now offer work-from-home arrangements to employees. Ninety percent of companies surveyed expect to have more employees working from home over the next 3 years."**

culture

I f it looks like a duck, walks like duck, and sounds like a duck, it must be a duck. Dave Hueller, CEO of the Eagle Learning Center, encourages personal responsibility and a no-excuses attitude toward getting the job done. Whenever anyone catches another employee, including Dave, making an excuse, the co-worker will good-naturedly start quacking. It is their way of trying to stay focused on solutions instead of finding blame.

▼   ▼   ▼

S outhwest Airlines is frequently cited as the company who has created the perfect blend of fun and humor for a successful business. Southwest tries to accommodate this interest in their success by hosting a quarterly meeting called "Southwest Culture Day" for people outside the organization. Here are some of the lessons Southwest shares with the attendees:

▼ Take the competition seriously, but not yourself.

fun

- ▼ Don't fear failure. Be creative, color outside the lines.

- ▼ Treat employees as families.

- ▼ Trust intuition and explore nutty ideas.

- ▼ Make your life and work adventurous.

- ▼ Celebrate everything.

- ▼ Have a sense of humor. Think funny, adopt a playful attitude, laugh at yourself.

▼   ▼   ▼

According to a *Wall Street Journal* article, Haworth Inc., of Holland, Michigan, has created a new chair called the Tas. It allows complete freedom of movement or "active sitting." According to Haworth, prolonged sitting creates a workforce that is slothful, unproductive, and unhealthy. Ergonomists have been saying for years that constant changes in a worker's seating pattern are needed to increase blood circulation, redistribute pressure on the spine and joints, and keep nerves active throughout the day.

culture

oretta LaRoche, international speaker and consultant in the area of stress management, and president of the company The Humor Potential, produces a newsletter for subscribers and clients called TADAH (The Association of Delightfully Alive Humans).

Here are Loretta LaRoche's

TEN TADAHS
FOR LIVING A STRESS-FREE LIFE

I live in gratitude.

I play along the way.

I renew myself daily.

I see the humor in myself.

I laugh at myself, not others.

I am joyfully in the moment.

As long as I show up I'll have fun.

For every obstacle there is a solution.

I enjoy others for who and what they are.

At work or at home, I am healthy, happy, and fit.

fun

The Humor Potential Inc., a Loretta LaRoche Company, produces a fun catalog of resources, products, and seminars for stress management. To contact The Humor Potential, phone 1-800-99-TADAH (800-998-2324), or visit Loretta online at www.LorettaLaRoche.com.

▼ ▼ ▼

D r. Gary Krane, author of the book *Simple Fun for Busy People*, suggests some easy activities for people to put more fun into their work. One game he calls Elevator Roulette. You play the game as you and your co-workers enter an elevator. As the doors close everyone starts singing a song. The first one to stop singing when the doors open gets to buy lunch. It's kind of a vertical musical chairs.

Another work-related game that Dr. Krane describes is played at Ben & Jerry's. Whenever anyone says the word *serious* (or a synonymous word), everyone must put on Groucho Marx glasses. Krane believers that this simple game helps keep meetings from becoming too serious. Oops!

culture

67

▼   ▼   ▼

DAVE'S TOP TEN LIST OF
MOST ADMIRED
FUN COMPANIES

Southwest Airlines

Ben & Jerry's

Sun Microsystems

Almost any dot.com company

Disney

Cisco Systems

BMC Software

Microstrategy

LEGO

BreakPoint Books and More
(Okay, it's my own company, but
we have a lot of fun.)

FUN FOCUS

A FUN FAIRY TALE

"Once upon a time (well, actually 1981), there was a professor named Dr. Robert Shillman who taught at the Massachusetts Institute of Technology (M.I.T.) near Boston. Dr. Bob, as he likes to be called, came up with a really neat idea: he decided to invent computers that can actually 'see.' He dreamed about how these computers, which he called machine vision systems, would be used in the automated factories of the future to gauge, guide, inspect and identify all kinds of products while they were being made."

Taken from the Cognex Activity Book, better known in financial circles as an annual report

COGNEX ENVISIONS FUN

When the concept of Fun at Work was still an oxymoron, Dr. Robert J. Shillman founded Cognex upon the core values of working hard. Nineteen years later, that philosophy continues to drive the success of the machine vision system manufacturer, which has grown into a world leader in its industry. Motivated by the dream of creating an environment that would combine entrepreneurship with entertainment, Shillman left the dry world of academia at MIT and Tufts in 1981. Using his own seed money, ideas gleaned from his studies of the brain, and the expertise of two MIT graduate students (who took time off to build the company's first optical character recognition machine), he made the leap of faith into the business world. Under Shillman's imaginative leadership, Cognex has survived—and thrived—in the

culture

brutal shakeout of an industry that has dwindled from 100 competitors in the eighties to only six today. Cognex now has more than 600 employees at locations around the world, and a continuing record of growth and profitability. Adopting many Japanese business concepts, Dr. Bob retains a crystal-clear company vision that is serious in its focus on quality, customer satisfaction, and commitment to corporate goals. Yet, his unconventional leadership style and often zany motivational methods help keep employee morale high and turnover extremely low in today's tight job market.

INVASION OF THE COGNOIDS

Take dress, for example. Depending on his mood or a special occasion, you could find Shillman dressed as a court jester for a magazine cover or as the Good Humor Man, generously distributing

Cool Cash employee bonuses from the back of an ice-cream truck. He's also made appearances as The Big Cheese, The Top Dog, and a Big Wheel. He readily admits that Halloween is his favorite holiday, so it's a firm corporate policy that everyone join in the fun by dressing up each year. The corporate dress code is also casual every day, and Cognex has even designed its own clothing line called Cogwear, which can be worn instead of traditional business attire anytime. And then, there are the company traditions. They begin with the recognition of all employees as Cognoids. There's a company anthem, taught to all new employees and sung at all company meetings and events, as well as a corporate salute that is performed by placing the right

fun

hand vertically on the bridge of the nose while intoning "To Preserve and Enhance" (the vision).

Cognex offers all of the typical employee incentives, such as a 401(k) plan and educational allowances, but enhances the compensation package with an array of innovative rewards designed to reinforce corporate traditions, celebrate success, and build a winning team spirit. President's Awards, which can range from bonuses of $1,000 to $10,000, are given annually to those who exceed expectations in terms of performance, attitude, and commitment to excellence, and company-wide bonuses are distributed when Cognex attains its annual corporate goals. Perseverance is one of the company's values, so longevity is rewarded with Perseverance Awards, unique gifts that include a special pin and an all-expense-paid getaway to a popular U.S. vacation destination at five years, extravagant week-long vacations to exotic international locations—and a 10-day vacation to a choice of one of the Wonders of the World locations on 15-year anniversaries.

FUN FOR ALL, AND ALL FOR FUN!

But that's not all. The company hosts elaborate annual summer outings for employees and their families, with outrageous themes like "Rockin' in the Fifties," which featured a 40-foot jukebox, a malt shop, and a team of hairdressers who gave each guest a Fifties do. One outing, called the "Summer Beach Blast," showcased performers Jan and Dean. There is an annual holiday formal event, along with regular after-work socials and

culture

a bi-monthly Night at the Movies, when the company rents a theatre for employees

and their families. Employees can customize their work areas using a special allowance, take a break from their computers to play sports outdoors, get in shape at the onsite fitness center, or feast in the company cafeteria on specially priced meals and snacks. There is even the unique COGMAP Mortgage Assistance Program that helps employees purchase homes.

The surprise factor is a major Cognex specialty. Consider the Thursday before the Fourth of July, when an unexpected Friday off was announced along with an extra $100 in cash, a beach bag, a beach ball, and a beach umbrella for everyone.

LEADERSHIP

FUN FROM THE TOP DOWN

FUN FROM THE TOP DOWN

When I speak to groups, their most common question is "How do I start having fun at work? My boss (manager, supervisor, owner, co-worker, fill-in appropriate person) is not a fun person." Let's face it: there are | fun | | people | , and there are people who prefer to make our life miserable. Maybe it is their way of having fun. But at some point you and I need to take some responsibility for our work environment and how we would like to interact with our co-workers.

Leadership does not necessarily imply a position of managerial authority. You can be a leader regardless of position or rank. To take the | lead |

in creating a fun workplace requires that you lead by *example*. Create your own atmosphere of fun within your own workspace. Take control of how you would like to work—the colors, sounds, toys—and encourage **others** to join. It has been my experience that the best champions of fun have the sort of magnetic personality that others like to be around. Why? Because they are fun!

It may sound simplistic, but it works. Start with yourself, start small, and encourage others **to** **join** the fun.

There are many examples of fun leaders who have created business empires, but I find the most intriguing stories to be those from individuals who put themselves on the top of **the** **fun** ladder.

F un-based leadership can improve a lot of the "soft" aspects of a workplace, like morale and job appreciation, but good leaders know that it can also improve the hard productivity measures that affect the bottom line. Dawn Morrelli, of Honeywell, as reported in *Incentive* magazine, has proven that fun and productivity do measure up. Dawn, known as the "calendar girl," keeps two calendars: one measures time in the standard way, the other tracks the number of days saved when a project is completed ahead of schedule. When the staff approaches a holiday on the fictitious calendar she celebrates the occasion. She has been known to hand out Valentine's Day cards in August, Easter eggs in September, and New Year's greetings in midsummer. After five months of tracking days saved, Dawn's staff had completed enough early deliveries to observe two years' worth of holidays, and had helped raise Honeywell's on-time delivery rate from 75% to 87%. And besides, who wouldn't want to celebrate their favorite holiday three times a year!

▼   ▼   ▼

People just need to lighten up at work and learn to laugh at yourself and with others, but not _at_ others. A sense of humor is incredibly important, especially in high-stress situations.
Lyn Austin, East Idaho Federal Credit Union

▼   ▼   ▼

_S_outhwest Airlines is generally acknowledged as one of the most fun places to work in the world, and it is regularly recognized as one of the top 100 companies to work for in the United States. Much of the culture of fun at Southwest Airlines is derived from their leader, Herb Kelleher, a pioneer in the People First philosophy of management. In an industry known for its

leaders

customer service horror stories, Kelleher has created a customer service model. In an industry in which most airlines have shown losses for many years, Kelleher has shown a profit every year since 1973, two years after Southwest's inception.

Herb defines leadership by example. Friday is fun day at Southwest, where everyone is allowed to dress down, or up, based on personal inclination. Herb has been known to show up for work dressed as Elvis, Roy Orbison, and many other famous characters. From the outset, Kelleher has put his trust and his business in the hands of his employees. Before employee empowerment was a catch phrase for making people feel good about themselves and their work, Kelleher put substance behind the philosophy. He put the focus directly on his people. The human resources department is called the People Department; training and development became Southwest Airlines' University for People. Southwest was the first airline to offer shares in the company, and it used the letters LUV as its stock symbol.

Southwest has made a great effort to maintain its unique culture by hiring the right type of employee. There is no shortage of prospects who would like to work at Southwest but, in order to make the cut, you need to be a fun individual who smiles all the time. Trust in employees to do the right thing, trust that if employees have fun so will customers, and recognition that without the right people a service-based business has no hope of survival has created a culture that oozes loyalty to the company and to its leader. In a recent annual report, Kelleher notes the importance of an employee-first attitude: "While a number of airlines may attempt to imitate Southwest, none of them can duplicate the spirit, unity, can-do attitudes, and marvelous esprit de corps of the Southwest employees, who continually provide superb customer service to each other and to the traveling public." Herb concludes his summary: "P.S. Our people are also a heck of a lot of fun to be with!"

Here are some tips from Southwest Airlines on how to create a fun culture (from *Customer*

leaders

79

Service Management, May/June 1999, by Tony Mosely):

- ▼ Don't let anyone frown on fun.
- ▼ Every level should join in.
- ▼ Specifically recruit fun people.
- ▼ Give people the freedom to create fun.
- ▼ Include entertaining the customer as part of people's jobs.
- ▼ Celebrate successes and anniversaries all the time.

▼ ▼ ▼

Everyone has a different leadership style, just as every organization has its own culture. Behaving in an appropriate manner, congruent with the accepted norms, is the challenge for leaders trying to make fun a part of their organization. Linda Erlich, owner of the Jeneric

fun

Group, a consulting company based in Detroit, Michigan, shows up to her place of work wearing bunny teeth and squirting co-workers who are tensing up under the pressure of a deadline. Her style fits her organization perfectly, and her employees thrive in this culture. Thirteen-year employee Marilynn Fox had her car keys hidden on her last work day before going on vacation. Throughout the day, Erlich gave her clues to finding her keys. Says Fox, "It energizes you. That laughter kind of gives you that deep breath you need to complete your day." (*Detroit Free Press*, 5/22/99)

▼   ▼   ▼

Many of our corporate leaders come from the numerous graduate schools throughout the world that offer advanced degrees in management. Although there is yet to be an

MBA in workplace fun (maybe I should start a program), one school is at least putting a little fun into the classroom. At Vanderbilt University in Nashville, in order to graduate with an MBA you must take Fred Talbott's communication class. In order to pass the communication class every student is required to do a stand-up comedy routine. "It requires the ultimate quality of a good speaker," shares Talbott. "I want them leaving here not taking things too seriously, having fun and infusing humor where they go."

As leaders, we are sometimes called to speak in front of an audience. Humor can be a great way to warm up an audience or to break up a long speech. If you are looking for that perfect joke (make sure it's appropriate) you might want to check out the website www.clari.net/rhf. According to *Internet World*, this site has some of the best humorous stories and jokes on the web.

fun

S ometimes people need new words to reflect the goings-on in the workplace. Here are some new words from Carolyn Thompson, of Training Systems of Frankfurt, Illinois, from her consulting experiences:

▼ **Blamestorming**. Sitting around in a group discussing why a deadline was missed or a project failed, and who was responsible.

▼ **Ohnosecond.** The minuscule fraction of time in which you realize that you've just made a big mistake (created a big opportunity, for you positive thinkers).

▼ **Flight risk.** Term used to describe employees who are suspected of planning to leave a company soon.

▼ **Seagull manager.** A manager who flies, makes a lot of noise, craps on everything, and then leaves.

Here are a few more words I've come across in the current work environment:

▼ **Salmon day.** A day spent swimming upstream, only to get nowhere in the end.

- ▼ **Cube farm.** An office where there are rows of cubicles instead of private offices.

- ▼ **Prairie dog.** A result of the cube farm. The prairie dog will pop his head above the cubicle wall to see what his officemates are doing.

- ▼ **Bandwidth.** The ability to take on a new project or meet a deadline.

▼   ▼   ▼

Many managers keep files on the mistakes and shortcomings of their employees in order to have documentation if a problem occurs and the employee needs to be terminated. Although legally it may be a prudent step, a more positive approach would be to keep a success file. This is a file folder of all the things your people do well, and a record of their successful endeavors. You can pull the file out at review time for a performance appraisal or even when you need that reminder of why you hired someone. The success file can include letters from grateful customers or recommendations and kudos from co-workers. Include pictures of the

fun

individual having fun at company functions or working hard in a training session. The file will become a unique documentation of why each person is special and value to your organization.

▼   ▼   ▼

Treat people as though they were what they ought to be and you help them become what they are capable of being.   **Goethe**

▼   ▼   ▼

S tore meetings are a regular occurrence at many retail-based businesses. It is management's chance to promote certain products, acknowledge an employee who has done a good job, or address problem areas. At a Wal-Mart store in Pasadena, Texas, store meetings are this and a whole lot more. Store manager Bradley Coonfield not only takes his weekly meetings to discuss the store's performance but he also uses the pep rally to allow department managers to

share information and success stories. According to Christopher Palmeri, of *Continental* magazine, toy-department manager Kimberley McCuiston has even brought her children to store meetings to help show how a certain product appeals to kids. Coonfield will lead the group in a guessing game of how many units a particular item has done over the past week.

The game promotes camaraderie and a sense of fun. The pep rally ends with the company cheer: "Give me a W, give me an A, . . ." The cheer ends with "Who's Number One?" The answer: "The customer!"

▼   ▼   ▼

The 9 to 5 job is pretty much gone, and people are increasingly busy. As a result, we're looking for fun and entertainment in every aspect of our lives.

Michael J. Wolf, *The Entertainment Economy*

fun

If you lead through fear you will have little to respect, but if you lead through respect you will have little to fear.   **Anonymous**

▼   ▼   ▼

According to George Fuller, author of *The Supervisor's Big Book of Lists,* there are four ways to reward employees without spending any money:

1. Let them set their own schedules. Let employees use their own judgment about when they take breaks and how long lunch should be.

2. Find advancement opportunities for them. Look for opportunities within and outside your own department. You may lose a good employee but your employees will realize that you care about their future as much as your own.

3. Give them plum assignments. Offer assignments that provide a change of pace, or allow them to sit on a special committee.

leaders

4. Praise them in front of their peers. There isn't a human being born who doesn't appreciate public praise.

Fun is missing from many companies. Now, noting a study by OfficeTeam, a staffing company from Menlo Park, California, I know why. The survey indicates that the effective communication present in most fun companies is actually missing from most companies in general. According to their nationwide study, only 38% of the surveyed employees felt comfortable approaching their boss. Only 44% thought their boss was willing to hear them out, and 15% felt their boss's door was firmly closed. "Good suggestions can come from all levels of the organization, and employees who interact regularly with clients or vendors can offer especially valuable feedback for improving products and services," says Diane Domeyer, of OfficeTeam.

fun

CEO Kris Horner, of Auto Glass Plus in Carrollton, Texas, knows that a day at the beach can really pump up the troops. Unfortunately, getting to the beach from landlocked Carrollton is kind of tough, so instead he brings a little of the beach to the office on Hawaiian Day. Aloha shirts, virgin daiquiris, and floral leis are the order of the day for this once-a-quarter activity that, Kris thinks, really helps to reduce the stress in the office. If you think a little island atmosphere is just for fun, think again. Auto Glass Plus reports an increase in sales of 5% to 25% on their tropical theme days. Kris, who spends the day delivering pizza and drinks to his employees, says it is a great way to connect with individuals: "You spend a bit of time talking to them and, as a business owner, I learn a lot. Without leadership involvement, it's just lunch." (Julie Sturgeon, "Fun Sells," *Selling Power*, March 2000) The theme days have become something the entire company has gotten behind. The employees volunteer their own time over the weekend to help decorate the office. The surf's up at Auto Glass Plus!

leaders

very leader needs to recognize the achievements of co-workers—and occasionally you may have to point out when they have dumbed something up. In my office we take the opportunity to recognize everyone's efforts at our staff meetings. At the beginning of the meeting, I share a success story about someone who made some magic happen over the last month. This person gets to wear a headband that I picked up at Disney World. This headband has Mickey Ears and his Cap for the Sorcerer's Apprentice. The employee who has shown the most creativity and fun over the past month gets to wear the Goofy Ears headband, and person who is in my doghouse gets to wear the Pluto Ears headband. I am the one wearing Pluto Ears most often.

Trust is a leader's most powerful tool; with it, a leader can build an achieving, lasting community; without it, the leader cannot build anything exceptional or lasting "
Dr. Leonard Berry, *Discovering the Soul of Service*
(Simon & Schuster, New York, 1999)

fun

DAVE'S TOP TEN LIST OF
THEME DAYS

**Hawaiian Day (because half my wardrobe
is Aloha shirts)**

Disco Day (or Seventies Day)

Clash Dressing Day

Bring Your Pet to Work Day

Disney Character Day

Movie Character Day

Formal Dress Day (tuxedos and long dresses)

Rock Star Day

Massage Day

Bring Children to Work Day

▼ ▼ ▼

It's kind of fun to do the impossible.

Walt Disney

leaders

ndrew Raskin reported, in e-diaries of *Inc.* magazine (August 2000), on his efforts to create a fun culture in his new venture, Gazooba Corp. of San Francisco, an Internet business that rewards visitors who refer friends to its sites. Andy handed all 16 employees $100 and told them to find fun stuff for the office. They ended up with foot scooters, enough helium-filled balloons to fill an office, and a large metal gong, which they now use to announce new customers and new employees. On another day at the office, when the afternoon called for an impulsive, ridiculous, off-the-wall infusion of fun (and Andy was just the guy to do it), they convinced a hot dog vendor to drag her cart from the street up to their offices. The cart wouldn't fit through the office door, so everyone lined up in the hall for Haagen-Dazs bars and franks.

▼   ▼   ▼

Imagination is intelligence having fun.

Anonymous

fun

Jana Nicol uses a special anti-stress kit when she comes up against bureaucratic un-fun thinking. The anti-stress kit is a sheet of paper taped to a wall, with the caption "Bang Head Here!" I hope she doesn't need to use the kit very often.

▼   ▼   ▼

The senior managers of FCC National Bank of Wilmington, Delaware, have been cooking up some fun. After a discussion led by a consultant, the management team was let loose in a kitchen with instructions and ingredients for a gourmet lunch. According to Faye Dadzie, vice president of human resources, "It really did simulate a work situation. Some instructions were incomplete. Sometimes we'd find ourselves working separately when we should have been working together to get the meal done on time." The team found new ways to work together and, to top it off, they got to sample the results of their team work. (**L.A. Times**, 9/14/97)

leaders

For employers who have made a point of hiring creative, talented, and intelligent people, there is a great book that will help your employees function better at work. *When Smart People Work for Dumb Bosses: How to Survive in a Crazy and Dysfunctional Workplace,* by William and Kathleen Lundin (McGraw-Hill, 1998). There is no better way to show your co-workers how much you value them than a book that shows how human you can be.

We try hard to keep a balance of seriousness and enjoyment. You get a different sense of your executives when you see them riding a tricycle in a race, then see them in the hall. You know they are real human beings.

> Cara Jane Finn, vice president of employee services, Remedy Corp. (*San Francisco Examiner*)

A toy box is something many companies are using at work to maintain a fun, playful work environment. If you are just starting to put you box together, humor consultants Marv and Mary Glaser of Omaha, Nebraska have a few ideas to help you:

▼ **Reading material**. Funny books, silly calendars, magazines, or scrap books.

▼ **Games.** Old standbys like checkers, bingo, dominos. Also include puzzles and brain teasers.

▼ **Creative toys.** Crayons, an instant camera, stickers, colored markers, construction paper, scissors, tape, building blocks, play money, pipe cleaners, sidewalk chalk.

▼ **Action toys.** Yo-yos, Frisbees, jump rope, a kite, balloons, squeezable stress toys, and Nerf or Koosh balls.

▼ **Electronic toys.** CD player (with appropriate music), humorous and inspirational tapes, and even a head-and-neck massager.

leaders

FINDING THE WORD ON LEADERSHIP

Are we learning to lead, or are we leadership challenged? A scan of the available books on leadership could lead you to believe that there are infinite successful models for managing an organization. This might be true! Successful leadership styles vary as much as personalities. Attempts have been made to measure and quantify each of them. Just for fun, I thought I would try to determine how many different books are available on leadership. Since I believe you can turn

just about any activity into a game, see how many of the seventeen leadership titles you recognize in the following Fun Forum.

LEADERSHIP FOR THE TWENTY-FIRST CENTURY

According to the executive search firm Christian and Timbers, the character traits of the most sought-after corporate leaders are drastically changing. Where past leaders were judged on traditional criteria, such as education, professional skills, and experience, the new science of leadership blends a contradictory mixture of skills. Phil Leggiere writes: "Practical experience is blended with long-term vision. The ability to wield power is balanced with sensitivity, and hardheaded realism is tempered with intuitive people skills." Like most successful companies, successful leaders have similar personality attributes. Since leadership success is difficult to measure, the Hagberg Consulting Group has developed a general profile of the best leaders: "The best leaders are perceived as having highly developed interpersonal skills. They are warm, open, and forthright, and their attitude toward employees is characterized by words like 'empowering,' 'supportive' and 'benevolently paternalistic.' They are able to balance the demand to get things done with sensitivity to the feelings of others. They try to foster teamwork through trust and commitment to widely shared team goals." Trust and communication skills are the keys to success when creating a fun workplace—or the leader of the future.

One of the first rules of leadership is to lead by example, but how do we awaken the leader within? There are wonderful companies whose CEOs tend to set the tone for office success. One of these timeless leaders is Jack

Kahl, former president and CEO of Manco, a manufacturer of duct tape. Kahl recognizes that leadership is a hands-on job. Each year Jack challenges the sales force to meet higher and higher sales goals. Realizing that goal-setting alone won't motivate his people, Jack exploits leadership secrets like a rogue warrior and calls on the competitive nature of the team. His challenge: When the sales team meets the goal, Jack swims across the company pond. If the sales team comes up short, they get to don *their* swimsuits for a dip. It may sound easy to those of you from warm climates, but an October pond in northern

leaders

Ohio would intimidate an Eskimo. The sales team accepted his challenge and exceeded the expectations of their transformational leader. Jack ceremoniously swam a length of the pond wearing only his favorite Speedo. The challenge created so much interest and enthusiasm that it has become an annual event that the entire company, and even the local community, have come to anticipate. "Trust allows us to have fun," says Kevin Krueger, director of education at Manco. "Our customers, our suppliers, and our partners enjoy working with us, which in the end helps to build our business." Trust and communication are characteristics that flow straight from Jack Kahl.

PRINCIPLE-CENTERED LEADERSHIP

One of the qualities employees admire most in a leader is an empowering attitude. To create an empowering atmosphere, start with values-based leadership. Holly Halvorson, of Colorado Trust in Denver, has a special way of leading from the heart. Holly uses four simple rules:

- Inject self-deprecation into every conversation, so that laughter starts with yourself.
- Play with words instead of people.
- Encourage people to laugh at their mistakes.
- Promote telling success stories, no matter how small.

Holly realizes that it is the small things done successfully on a daily basis that create an environment that fosters teamwork, creativity, and productivity. It's a lot like following the Golden Rule.

fun

UN-ENLIGHTENED LEADERSHIP

Scott Adams, author of *The Dilbert Future*, is excellent at pointing out the absurdities of corporate leadership. In his latest book he retells an allegedly true story. "At one technology company, senior management became angered that two important projects had been named Ren and Stimpy, after famous cartoon characters. They declared that henceforth there would be a master namer who would approve the names of all future projects. The master namer would choose from a list of famous river names to ensure appropriate and dignified names. The process worked well until engineers presented the status of projects Ubangi and Volga. Senior management was livid until someone explained that those are names of rivers." It's a funny story, but how many leaders do we recognize in those managers? Toxic leaders can poison the energy, creativity, and, ultimately, the productivity from any organization.

I believe that success as a leader is determined by our ability to balance the demands of hard strategic management with sensitivity to the feelings of others. Success or failure is like riding a leadership trapeze.

FOR THOSE OF YOU KEEPING SCORE

If you were keeping track, I used seventeen titles in this article. Here they are, in the order used:

- *Learning to Lead*, Bennis
- *Leadership Challenge*, Kouzes and Posner
- *Leadership for the Twenty-First Century*, Rost
- *Leadership and the New Science*, Wheatley
- *Lead to Succeed,* Patino
- *Leader of the Future*, ed. Hesselbein
- *Awaken the Leader Within*, Perkins
- *Timeless Leader*, Clemens
- *Leadership Secrets of the Rogue Warrior*, Marcinko

leaders

- *Transformational Leader*, Tichy
- *Principle-Centered Leadership*, Covey
- *Values-Based Leadership*, Kuczmarski
- *Leadership from the Heart*, Meyer
- *Enlightened Leadership*, Oakley
- *Toxic Leaders*, Whicker
- *On Becoming a Leader*, Bennis
- *Leadership Trapeze*, Wilson.
- (I am not going to count *The Dilbert Future* by Scott Adams because technically it isn't a leadership title.)

There were probably many titles that I included by accident. When I did the search for business books on leadership, I came up with over 1000 titles published since January 1998. I guess there is a lot to say on the subject.

CUSTOMER SERVICE

PRIORITY FUN

CUSTOMER SERVICE

PRIORITY FUN

Isn't it always more pleasurable to do business with someone who has the ability to lighten, as well as enlighten, a situation? Now, I am not suggesting that customer service isn't SERIOUS business—you know it is. But what I am suggesting is that, when customers can feel comfortable with a customer-caring representative of your company, they will have more trust and confidence in the whole company. Often, an easy way to build that bridge of understanding is through the human sharing of the common need for joy. When you ask people to recount some of the most pleasurable experiences of their lifetimes, they often tell of times when they were having fun—times when they laughed together with others, shared a chuckle, were amused or lightened by the same perspective of a situation. Humor is used to bond with others, to lighten the heavy load of living, and to relieve stress.

In our day-to-day interactions with customers and colleagues there may be many opportunities to have fun. They can be spontaneous or elaborately planned. Either way, they make the experience more enjoyable and more memorable—and isn't that *what you* are *after, experiences both your staff and your customers will remember fondly? If customer service, or better yet, customer-caring is your business, then read on and discover the many ways you can create the* fun *experiences that make people smile, laugh, and want to come back and do business with you.*

JoAnna Brandi

Like many companies, the Mirage Hotel and Casino in Las Vegas, Nevada, likes to keep current with any and all customer service requests and complaints. Also like many companies, when staff is short, work may pile up. In order to keep current, the customer service department holds a Skeleton in the Closet party. I know that there must be numerous skeletons in the closets of Las Vegas, but at the Mirage what they are looking for is the oldest unresolved customer service complaint. All the employees are encouraged to bring out their skeletons and together they resolve the complaint. Prizes are awarded for the oldest resolved complaint at the party. This is a great way to overcome the natural human tendency to procrastinate on difficult or old work.

For anyone who travels regularly, the FAA instructions given to airplane passengers prior to takeoff have to be the most ignored set of instructions ever uttered. On a recent America West flight the flight attendant not only had everyone's complete attention but we were also virtually on the edge of our seats, straining to hear every word. This creative employee revised the entire FAA instructions to fit the poem "The Night Before Christmas" by Clement Moore:

> *'Twas the flight before Christmas, and*
> *all through the plane*
> *Not a passenger was stirring, because*
> *their*
> *Seat belts were fastened and tray*
> *tables raised.*

This clever attendant recited the entire poem much to enjoyment and applause of the passengers.

And to all a good flight!

America West has more than one humorist among its flight attendants. Another fun-loving flyer recently tuned in just as the flight attendant intoned: "When the oxygen masks drop, just put a quarter in the slot and then place the mask over your nose and mouth."

service

The best way to have a good idea is to have a lot of ideas.   **Dr. Linus Pauling**

▼   ▼   ▼

As service professionals, we are trained not to use the word *no*. But, try as we may, we tend to overuse this creativity-crushing word. According to Dartnell's *Team Leader*, it is not unusual for people to say *no* as much as 50 times a day. A fun exercise to help stifle the *nos* is to document each time you say *no*, and then try to change it to a *maybe*. Saying *maybe* allows for creative ideas to percolate and take you down new creative avenues.

▼   ▼   ▼

For a lot of great ideas on customer service improvement, check out *Customer Service Management* magazine. For more information, visit their website at www.csm-us.com.

fun

The Orange County Transportation Authority in Orange, California, really walks its talk about having a fun workplace. Or, should I say, they really know how to drive the fun bus. The president of OCTA showed up in a crown (as Queen of the office) at a recent company-wide meeting, and training videos have included dancing to the Village People song "YMCA" using O-C-T-A.

The president told me of a customer service training they were about to do. She feels strongly that management needs to walk a mile in the shoes of their customers if they are continually to improve their service. OCTA developed a unique and fun way to do this. At an upcoming training session, all middle- and upper-level managers are to be loaded on a bus as if they are going to an offsite training retreat. Where they will actually be headed is to every conceivable location throughout the county. All of the employees will be individually dropped off, with a bus schedule

service

in hand, and told to find their way back to the office using only public transportation. Bus drivers will be required to sign all transfers just in case someone decides they might want to take a taxi back to the office. This is an excellent idea for an organization's employees to get a greater understanding of the service they provide and the customers that they serve.

▼ ▼ ▼

An employee at a Palo Alto medical clinic wants to make the time people spend at the clinic as short and stress-free as possible. When children come into the clinic for vaccinations, she finds that distracting them by having fun makes the actual injection go more smoothly and easily for the children. She has been known to sit down on the waiting room floor and blow bubbles or play games with inflated balloons.

You want to be more customer friendly? Then close the doors of your customer service departments! Just shut 'em down! Everybody does customer service, not just a department.

Tom Peters

▼   ▼   ▼

The zany culture prevalent at Southwest Airlines is well documented. As a company, Southwest has consistently won the industry triple crown (best on-time performance, best baggage-handling accuracy, and best-rated customer service). The success of Southwest's service ratings can be attributed to the myth-shattering attitude of the customer being #2. At Southwest, the *employees* are #1. According to Orvel Ray Wilson, co-author of *Guerilla Selling,* the whole office has been known to shut down to celebrate birthdays and anniversaries. CEO Herb Kelleher's philosophy is simple: "If you take care of your people, they will take exceptional care of your customers." The walls of the offices are lined with photographs and memorabilia from

service

company events that range from Halloween parties to award ceremonies. Wilson writes: "This self-promotion creates a unique esprit de corps, which everyone here refers to as The Southwest Spirit. It's an energy that fuels everything they do. And they do it better than anyone else in the sky."

▼   ▼   ▼

A game recently brought to my attention is called the Six Degrees of Kevin Bacon. From what I understand, this activity has been around for a while, but it's new to me. Doug Grove, my co-worker at BreakPoint Books, introduced the game to me while working at a convention. As anyone who has worked a convention knows, it is extremely difficult to maintain a high level of service throughout an entire conference without some activity to keep your spirits up. Basically, this game is a mental exercise in which you try to come up with connections between actors and actresses that will bring you to a movie in which the actor Kevin Bacon has acted. For example, if I say Robert Redford, Doug would find a connection to Kevin Bacon. Robert Redford was in *The Sting* with Paul Newman, Paul Newman was in *The Color of Money* with Tom Cruise, Tom Cruise was in *A Few Good Men* with Kevin Bacon. From what I am told, you can get from virtually any performer to Kevin Bacon within six movies. I know I'm not that good.

▼   ▼   ▼

Goofing off is in the eye of the beholder. What one person sees as goofing off is another person rejuvenating themselves, someone who's likely to do a better job at work in an hour than someone who's holding in lots of tension.

Matt Weinstein, president of Playfair Inc.

service

D r. Jeff Alexander, founder of Gentle Dental and Youthful Tooth, knows that health professionals have a reputation of being a little boring, so he has created an atmosphere that fosters fun for both employees and patients. "We look for any excuse to remember there's a child inside us who has to play." According to Gillian Flynn, of the *San Francisco Examiner*, each morning the employees in the dental offices "huddle" and "recommit," sharing laughs and good news. "Throughout the day, employees who are feeling low can call huddles. Whoever's not working heads over to trade a joke or a humorous thought." Dr. Alexander feels these gatherings help employees release tension and refocus on their work, instead of stewing all day. The bottom line in a dental office is to keep the employees stress-free and happy, so that the patients can stay stress-free and happy too.

▼　　▼　　▼

A ll service professionals' workplaces may not lend themselves to a dress-down or casual-dress day. Many salespeople, because of their company, position, or industry, must maintain a professional appearance at all times. For salespeople in these positions, Wayne Eagles of Pearl Assurance PLC in England, suggests an "underground dress code" for a bit of fun. Based on the color of the shirt you are wearing, you can tell the mood of the individual wearing the shirt (kind of like mood rings for the sales profession). Wayne's secret code is:

Blue   I've had a bad week, so cheer me up.
Pink   I'm working with a difficult group this week.
Green   I'm working with a brilliant group this week.
White   I'm on a tight deadline this week. Do not disturb me.
Yellow   It's Friday!

▼   ▼   ▼

JoAnna Brandi, author of the *The Customer Care Lady's Bi-Weekly Tip,* an e-mail newsletter, has several tips for getting your employees and co-workers excited and energized about caring for customers:

▼ Get out of your office and into the customer's. Allow people to see and experience how your product fits into their life.

▼ Bring 'em to you. Invite customers to visit frequently.

▼ Tell stories, take pictures. Take a picture of customers using your product.

▼ Have customers run a meeting. Let them pick the topic and design and agenda.

▼ Send the staff shopping. Let your staff go out and be someone else's customer with the express purpose of evaluating service.

▼ Celebrate a Customer Day. Have one every month. Celebrate a client's successes and achievements.

▼   ▼   ▼

To receive *The Customer Care Lady's Bi-Weekly Tip,* **contact JoAnna Brandi at Ecare@emailch.com.**

fun

Who could resist the opportunity to have a six-foot mouse clean your teeth? That is what dental hygienist Patty Hastreiter, of Lancaster, New York, did on Disney Day at the dental office where she works. "Everyone was dressed in their Disney finest. Prizes were awarded for best character, best accessory, and best overall Disney theme. Minnie Mouse, Pocahontas, Cinderella, and some Mouseketeers reported for work that morning! Our patients loved it." (*Disney* magazine, Fall 2000) This is a great idea that can be used regardless of your favorite cartoon character. You can have Warner Brothers Day, and work with Bugs Bunny or Daffy Duck—or how about Flintstones Day, where people dress up like Fred, Wilma, Barney, and Betty? Bringing back memories of our childhood is a lot of fun for both customers and co-workers.

▼　　▼　　▼

Fun is about as good a habit as there is . . .
Jimmy Buffett, *A Pirate Looks at Fifty*
Random House, 1998

service

DAVE'S TOP TEN LIST OF
FUN OFFICE TOYS

Silly Slammers

**(those toys that say something
when you drop them)**

Nerf guns (balls, arrows, etc.)

Yo-yos

Squishy stress balls

Slinky

Koosh ball (and all the other Koosh products)

Foosball table

Video games (Sega, Nintendo, etc.)

Silly Putty

Ping-Pong tables

Mary and Marv Glaser are corporate trainers and occupational humorists who are often asked how to integrate healthy humor into lives. They use a clever puzzle to answer the question.

Assign a number to each letter below based on its position in the alphabet:

A T T I T U D E

___ ___ ___ ___ ___ ___ ___ ___

Add all the numbers together = _____ %

The answer is 100% attitude.
Our ability to respond or react to life's challenges relies on our positive attitude.

▼   ▼   ▼

At NovaCare Rehabilitation, in Mayfield Village, Ohio, they have found that a combination of fun and games helps them to maintain and expand their customer base. According to Laura Sullivan, director of HR support services of the employees' resource council: "They feel that if their employees are having fun their customers will enjoy the experience as well." (*Cleveland Plain Dealer*, 9/24/00) NovaCare constantly runs contests that both the employees and the patients get to take part in. "When a patient comes to us, they are usually in pain," says NovaCare VP Deborah Singer. "We try to make something that may be scary and uncomfortable into something fun!"

▼　　▼　　▼

For people who spend a lot of time in chairs in front of computer monitors, like call center reps, it would be a real treat to leave the office and go to an amusement park to ride a roller coaster. Unfortunately, most businesses can't afford to shut down their call centers for a little offsite fun. An in-house alternative might just be the thing for these chairbound employees. Have a ride on a roller coaster without ever leaving the office!

Line up a group of chairs, preferably two by two. The leader, who "rides" in the first row, starts the ride, with all the others imitating the leader's every sound and move. You start the ride by going up a hill. "Click, click, click" the leader will chant, mimicking the sound of coaster train going up a hill. The leader should announce their arrival at the top, and with a pregnant pause, start shooting down the hill.

"AAAAAARRRRRRRG!" screams the leader, throwing her hands up in the air. A sharp turn to the left is at the bottom of the hill (hands up and to the left), now a turn to the right, and "AAAAAAAAAAHHHHHHHHHH!" (hands up and to the right). Now down another hill (hands straight up), and into a loop-the-loop, "AAAAAARRRRRRGH" (hands and arms making a big circle from above your head to your knees).

This is a really silly game, and it has some wonderful benefits. It is something that everyone can do without even leaving their workstation. It is a great exercise for lethargic times of the afternoon because it helps get the blood flowing. Most important, I have never seen anyone come off the roller coaster ride not smiling and giggling. It is really great fun. Ready to go up again?

service

RAIN FOREST CAR WASH, JUST ADD FUN

Fun at work is a concept that can extend well beyond your work environment or things that you do for your employees. Fun can be a key attribute of your core product or service. Entertainment value and fun can be a major differentiater for many products, but especially for a mundane commodity, service, or product. In fact, according to *The Experience Economy,* by B. Joseph Pine II and James Gilmore, "The delivery of basic goods and services is no longer enough for companies to provide their customers. Companies will succeed by providing something special or extra that adds value." Certainly, making your customers' experience fun and memorable is one important way to keep them coming back.

IT'S A JUNGLE OUT THERE

In the case of the Rain Forest Car Wash in Lafayette, Indiana, fun is the real product at this jungle-theme car wash. A clean car is just an ancillary benefit. The vision was inspired by Kendall Smith's many photographic tours of Central and South America. The mood is set immediately when customers enter the facility through giant stone arches to the melodious sounds of two waterfalls with Mayan images on the facing. From here customers can "adventure" to the self-wash area or explore the tunnel-wash option.

fun

through the jungle and elephants spray water from their trunks during the rinsing stage. After going below a rope bridge with snakes dangling from above, the final pause is made at the dark, exotic Mayan King's Cave of Treasure, where cars are dried.

In the self-wash, jungle sounds of birds and beasts, rain and storms, turn a dirty job into a sensory experience. But it is the tunnel-wash that provides the real thrill for adults and children alike. At the tunnel entrance, a large stone face is animated to welcome visitors with greetings such as "Don't feed the animals" or "Watch out for the creepy crocodile inside." The car proceeds to move through a forest filled with the shrieks and screams of animated animals including, among many, swinging monkeys and giant birds. A rainstorm punctuates the car's passage

KIDS ARE KINGS OF THE JUNGLE

"We provide a top-quality product, but we've offered another reason than just a clean car to come here," according to Kendall Smith. "Children are delighted by the experience and encourage their parents to come back again. In fact, kids are one of our major markets."

Kendall and his partner Steven Shook have spared no expense in the creation of this exotic venue, hiring nationally known architects, sculptors, landscapers, and animators to create

service

a first-class environment with the perfect ambiance. The unique concept has been such a smashing success that nationwide expansion is on the drawing board. I guess you could say that Kendall and Steven are cleaning up!

SALES & MARKETING

FUN SELLS

SALES & MARKETING

FUN SELLS

Even after the many years of not having to
cold-call office buildings or spend hours trying to
drum up business on the telephone, I still consider myself a salesman (sorry, sales*person*).
Anyone who has made a living selling
products or services knows in their heart that
they will never have to worry about having a job.
It is an exhilarating feeling to know that people
will spend their hard-earned money because of
you. And, as any good salesperson will tell you, it
is not the product they are buying, they are buying the salesperson.

Building a level of trust and understanding in a sales relationship **can** **be** difficult. The first step, typically, is to find common ground. As you will see in this chapter, many successful sales organizations are using fun as the common ground to build a relationship. Fun removes barriers, fun encourages participation, fun garners attention, fun builds trust, fun furthers understanding, fun can be memorable.

In your upcoming sales period—be it an annual, quarterly, or monthly objective—plan to use fun as a strategic tool. Determine the client and the strategy. Are you trying to educate the client or are you trying to gain some additional attention? Pick a client, pick a **fun** strategy, and get started using some of these fun ideas with your clients today.

R eactivating old accounts and opening new ones from sales reps' lists is a perpetual problem for virtually all sales managers. Sales reps are always fiercely protective of their prospect lists even if they have never called on, or have no intention of calling on, the prospects. This dilemma led a sales manager at a major radio station in Cleveland, Ohio to create an Account Draft Lottery. The sales force was allowed two weeks to study their prospect lists and identify five accounts that they wished to protect. After that, all prospects were up for grabs by the rest of the sales force. On the day of the draft, everyone dressed up in appropriate athletic attire. Each sales rep drew a draft number from a jar of numbered Ping-Pong balls. According to that order, each rep then selected 10 draft choices from the entire inactive-prospect account list. The sales manager set a goal of

$100,000 in new business in 3 months from the inactive list and put a large thermometer on the wall to track progress. The sales force blew by the goal in well under the time limit, so each member of the sales team was given a special, unexpected bonus.

▼   ▼   ▼

Jim O'Connell, LEGO System's senior vice president, uses his national and regional meetings for a little team building. "For the most part, salespeople are on their own. To me it's a reinforcement to have fun together." (Julie Sturgeon, "Fun Sells," *Selling Power*, March 2000) So, when the sales force does meet, Jim likes to maximize their fun time together by hosting beach Olympics, softball tournaments, and especially contests to determine the most creative use of the plastic LEGO bricks. Seasonal

sales

regional meetings include themes like October's "Monster Mash," November's "Turkey Trot," and December's "Festival of Displays." Jim feels that the fun meetings are a big benefit to building a cohesive, stress-free workforce. "The under-pinning of fun is trust. A team can relax and have fun when you balance the festivity with the honesty."

The World Wide Web is a tremendous resource for many professionals. Recently a resource for the sales profession has emerged as a tool for research, sales tools, and chat. Siebel has created sales.com for sales professionals to help improve their effectiveness and productivity. The site includes web-based tools for tracking and managing contacts, accounts, and competitors, and for finding new business opportunities. And it's a lot more fun than the Monday morning breakfast with your sales manager!

fun

Many companies offer drawings and other giveaways to entice prospective customers to visit their exhibit space in any of the thousands of conventions and expositions taking place around the world. A fun way to increase traffic and to increase the amount of times a prospect might come back is to call on everyone's creative flair. Try taking a blown-up photograph of something silly. Invite attendees to write captions, for the funny photo and post them next to the poster for all to see. Toward the end of the exposition, award prizes to the most creative and funny captions, and have the winners come back to your booth to pick up their prizes.

▼　　▼　　▼

Sales and marketing is about developing lasting relationships with your customers. A sense of humor and fun are two tools that should be in every person's sales kit. Barry Lee, president of Main Trucking and Rigging Company in

Elmwood Park, New Jersey, is a big proponent of this philosophy. "This is a high-pressure business, so when I see tension building I usually do something stupid." Something stupid might entail walking on his hands in the middle of a staff meeting. Lee is a prankster, not only in the office but also with his clients. According to *Sales & Marketing Management* magazine (March 1999), Lee likes to treat his accounts as if they were friends, calling them names, or calling them and pretending to be an

auditor from the Internal Revenue Service. He claims that the pranks help to create a closer bond with his customers. "Humor is important in life and in business," Lee says.

▼   ▼   ▼

great way to generate enthusiasm for your product or service is to have an annual contest for the most creative photograph or video of someone using your product. This is a fun way to generate interest and customer loyalty for your product and it is also a research tool to find new uses for existing products.

The Fly By Night Club in Anchorage, Alaska, has a nightly show called The Whale Fat Follies. The show has been running for years, appealing to both tourists and Alaskans. In the show, the entourage leader, Mr Whitekeys, encourages audiences to take pictures of themselves with a can of Spam in front of famous buildings, statues, and other landmarks from around the world and send them back to the club. These photographs are used in the show and also decorate the walls of the club. It is extremely interesting (and fun) to see what and where people have taken pictures of themselves with Spam. Spam at the U.S. Capitol, Spam at the Tower of Pisa. Spam covering places of the human anatomy. Spam around the world! If you are wondering why Spam is the canned meat of choice at The Fly By Night Club, it's because Alaska is the #1 per capita consumer of Spam in the United States. Way to go, Alaska!

sales

▼   ▼   ▼

DAVE'S TOP TEN LIST OF
FUN WEBSITES

pogo.com
espn.com
bluemountain.com
ebay.com
toysrus.com
candystand.com
buzztime.com
disney.com
nuttysites.com
(if you like dancing animals)
gamesville.com

Brian Pelletier, of Chicago, likes to use fun as a presentation prop. Brian uses children's hats to help make his points during a presentation. If he is relaying how his public relations firm handles a crisis, he wears a fireman's hat. If he is talking about his firm's teamwork, he wears a baseball cap. To symbolize herding the team in a collective direction, he will wear a cowboy hat. According to Brian after one meeting: "It went over great. The clients loved it and it really stuck in people's minds long after the meeting." Sounds like a great sales tool.

▼ ▼ ▼

Sales organizations have been known to spend thousands (if not millions) on giveaway trinkets and advertising specialty items at conferences and exhibitions. Katina Ho, a marketing representative for Level 8, a software company from Dulles, Virginia, likes to give away fun when promoting her company from the

sales

exhibit floor. Katina likes to give away tangles, an interesting promotional puzzle that advertises her company. "Toys don't get tossed when you get back to the office. They tend to be more memorable and are left on their desk longer." Katina adds, "and the techies love 'em." Besides the stress-relieving tangles, Katina likes to give out color-changing foam footballs in the fall. Katina concludes "I want to keep my name in front of our potential clients as much as possible, and fun toys help do that for me."

▼　　▼　　▼

Those who can't laugh at themselves leave the job to others.　　　　　　　　　**Anonymous**

▼　　▼　　▼

reg Zedlar, a senior financial advisor for American Express in Glendale, California, created his own line of greeting cards to help

fun

solicit new business. He came up with the idea about three years ago to open more doors and close more business. One card shows a bleak scene of a snow-covered graveyard. The caption reads "Someday we will both be dead," followed on the inside with "Let's do some business before it's too late." Another card reveals a shady-looking character with the advice "Fire your bookie," and inside "Hire a financial advisor." Zedlar feels the cards are a way to "strip the formality and let people see your personality." The overall response to the cards was so positive that he has started his own company called Conceptual Thinking Inc. in Burbank. (*Wall Street Journal*)

▼   ▼   ▼

In any business situation where you can interject appropriate humor, it helps break down stress and creates better relationships.

Peter Shevlin, sales manager,
Principal Financial Group,
in the *Las Vegas Review-Journal*, February 23, 1999

sales

According to *Incentive* magazine, Sprint's Dallas office has a great way to reward its sales staff for meeting sales goals. They have the Sprint version of Wheel of Fortune, where each successful salesperson gets to spin the wheel for prizes. Prizes include raffle tickets and afternoons off. This is an extremely easy way to get everyone involved in a fun project.

▼   ▼   ▼

Being called Gumby (dammit) might seem odd as a way to encourage and reward your salespeople, but at the Container Store it is the highest compliment you can receive. Being a Gumby means that you are flexible—that you go out of your way to help another worker or a customer.

Little and large Gumbys are on display at the Container Stores and at the headquarters. What a great way to reward special service—hand employees a flexible green toy and call them a Gumby!

fun

In case you missed it, October 24 is National Crazy Day, an annual challenge for offices to celebrate their silliness and to convince normally sedate CEOs and salespeople to bring out their wild side. *Sales and Marketing Management* magazine sponsors the annual event and awards prizes to the most innovative offices. Past winners include Marketing Innovators of Rosemont, Illinois, whose office workers wore their clothes backwards for the day. Other entrants hosted pajama parties and cow-mooing contests. Rachel Towle, of New York–based WalkerGroup/CNI, says "The event promoted a feeling of togetherness that is often lost among the day-to-day pressures of the workplace."

▼　　▼　　▼

By now everyone has heard of, if not participated in, casual Fridays (or any other day of the week, for that matter). Countering the trend, the Pollak Agency in Edison, New Jersey,

sales

has turned the tables on dressing down and created Formal Fridays. The advertising agency employees show up for work in tuxedos and evening gowns in hopes that they not only draw attention to themselves but also draw the attention of new customers.

A great resource for those of you who would like to add a little magic to your training is a book by Ed Rose, *Presenting and Training with Magic: 53 Simple Tricks You Can Use to Energize Any Audience* (McGraw-Hill, New York, $34.95).

A website article for the *Los Angeles Times* (1999) listed six ways to improve your creative thinking and imagination. Great tools for any sales fun-atic:

▼ Become a knowledge sponge. Bombard your mind with relevant information regarding your product, service, and market. Read books, watch videos, take part in sales training. You are dumping knowledge into your "mental Cuisinart," the conscious and subconscious mind.

▼ Become an explorer. Dare to escape from mundane habits. Take a new way to the office or to your accounts. Change your message. Find something new to share with clients. Sleep on the other side of the bed. Monotonous routine makes for monotonous thinking.

▼ Learn to play. Make time for mischief. Visit a toy store and pick out something that makes you or others laugh.

▼ Take "break-ations." Ward off dull thinking and dull performances by taking a mental vacation. Take a walk, meditate, do some deep breathing to recharge your batteries.

▼ Follow your rhythms. Find out when you are your most alert or when you typically are dragging. Plan your day around your own body's schedule. Do repetitive nonthinking jobs when you're low, and plan the day's biggest challenges around the high-energy times.

▼ Avoid "boo leaders." These are the naysayers, the people who like to drop Fun Bombs. Avoid their thinking, especially when you are still developing an idea.

▼   ▼   ▼

Wayne Eagles, of Pearl Assurance PLC in the United Kingdom, has brought his skills as a former magician to his current career of sales trainer. Every Friday afternoon he performs a couple of tricks for the other training designers. He encourages their participation by  having them try to figure out how the trick was done and by inviting them to bring their own tricks to share the following week. This is a great way to develop a person's powers of observation and demonstration skills.

S alespeople are always looking for recognition and rewards for jobs well done. One Virginia-based recreation company decided to honor these people by giving them their "just desserts." They created a build-your-own sundae bar and recognized all individuals for their contributions.

▼   ▼   ▼

A sense of humor, with tongue firmly in cheek, has helped Gundlach Bundschu Winery in Sonoma, California, differentiate themselves from the myriad of California Wine Country competitors. A visit to their tasting room is an experience for both the taste buds and the funny bone. The back wall of their tasting room has on display (and for purchase) posters and postcards of their many advertisements. One ad shows a vintage police car pulling over a driver. The caption reads "Sonoma sobriety test #1. If you can't say Gundlach Bundschu Gewurztraminer, you shouldn't be driving." A play on the movie *Field of Dreams* shows a near-empty baseball stadium.

sales

The caption reads "If you pour it they will come." All the stadium ads in the photograph have been replaced with Gundlach Bundschu ads. Long-time employee Doug Ross thinks it is the fun people have when visiting that keeps them coming back: "This is a great place to work, we have a lot fun with the people who come and visit." Not only are the ads fun, but so are the names of the wines and the art decorating the labels. My favorite (both name and taste) is the Polar Bearitage. You can visit their website at www.gunbun.com and check out the wide variety of their humorous advertisements and label art.

▼   ▼   ▼

Zany Brainy is proving that fun sells. The Wynnewood, Pennsylvania-based retailer of children's toys has gone from startup to 100 stores in 9 short years. The store's theme is "A Zillion Neat Things for Kids." CEO Keith Spurgeon credits Zany Brainy's growth to their unique sales strategy. "We want children to wander through the store, having fun, opening things." (*Playthings*, April 1999) Fun helps

fun

create an atmosphere where customers like to hang out. Fun does sell, but Zany Brainy gives it away free. They  even have a Free Fun Every Day program that is held in the store's theatre. The program varies from mini-concerts to artists demonstrating arts and crafts.

▼   ▼   ▼

Having fun is like being a good lover. It doesn't come naturally.

Gary Krane, *Simple Fun for Busy People*

▼   ▼   ▼

According to authors Nancy Michaels and Debbi Karpowicz, the best marketing ideas are off-the-wall. In their book *Off-the-Wall Marketing Ideas: Jump Start Your Sales Without Busting Your Budget* (Adams Media,

sales

1999), they show that the best ideas are inexpensive and easy. For example, use a miniature image of your product as a part of your name badge for the next business meeting you attend, or use your name to make it memorable. Marci Blaze, of Venice, California, singes the edge of her stationary to make an unforgettable tie to her name.

▼　　▼　　▼

The Macaroni Grill started a great program to drum up new customers: have them cook! The Macaroni Grill is now offering cooking lessons to individuals who want to improve their culinary skills. It is a great way to give people a special look into your restaurant and to develop a greater appreciation for the products you serve and the people who serve them. When the Macaroni Grill starts bartending lessons, I may be first in line.

You never know what odd or funny thing you or your company can become known for. National Discount Brokers (NDB), a New Jersey financial services company, has had a duck as its symbol for quite a while. The company's motto is "We Take You Under Our Wing."

In a recent attempt to streamline their voicemail systems they added a little fun. When calling their toll-free customer-service number, a caller will hear a menu of NDB's services. Option #7 is "If you would like to hear a duck quack, press 7." Yes, hear a duck quack. Pretty silly, huh? Before the duck-quack option, a normal day consisted of about 5000 incoming calls. The most recent accounting showed that the volume of calls has reached 300,000 per day. New customer acquisitions are also way up—a better indicator of the success of the quacking. Company spokesman Rich Tauberman says "People are happy a large company would do something like this. We haven't attached any promos. Our customers think it's nice when someone does something fun and frivolous."

THE ART DIRECTOR OF FUN

Art Sobczek was inspired by the idea of having fun at work when he was employed as marketing director at a very large corporation. The company was downsizing, and employee morale was at an all-time low. Art took it upon himself to implement some teambuilding exercises to lift everyone's spirits. He gave each of the teams 20 inches of tape, 20 straws, and a couple of raw eggs. The goal was to build a device that could hold the eggs without breaking. Many broken eggs later, employee attitudes had miraculously improved. This experience led him to incorporate humor and fun officially into his everyday worklife.

Currently, Art is a branch manager for Pacific Life Insurance, where he has adopted the motto that "Our mission is to help our agents make more money in less time by having more fun." The fun starts with Art, and his license plate reads CRE8 FUN. Art's attitude is evident in everything he does, from recruiting to the way he deals with customers and employees and the overall work environment.

RENAISSANCE ART

Before candidates for employment are given a formal application they are given a paper bag, full access to the office supply room, and 15 minutes to create a tangible description of themselves. Those who approach the challenge with creativity and zest go on to the next step in the hiring process, while those who take themselves too seriously are politely steered to the door.

Once you are part of the team, there is never a dull moment. Periodically, Art will

fun

announce Movie Friday, with a portion of the afternoon devoted to watching videos and munching on popcorn. Then there was the time he told everyone to dress in jeans and tennis shoes with no explanation. He took them to an upscale mall, rushed them to the top of the escalator and, at the stroke of noon, gave each an envelope with $100 in cash along with a 1-hour deadline to spend it all or lose it back to him. After blowing by the goals set during a 2-month sales challenge, employees were treated to a dinner and whirlyball, a lacrosse-type game played in the electric bump 'em cars found at amusement parks.

THE ART AND SCIENCE OF FUN

Anniversaries and promotions are always celebrated as special occasions. Recently Art pretended to ignore an anniversary and sent an employee on a rush errand to a large client. Art hid in the lobby and watched as the employee literally ran to the client's elevator. He jumped out to surprise her with an invitation to a special celebration lunch in the same building. For another anniversary, the employee was blindfolded and driven on a surprise trip through the city to his favorite restaurant. Stares and shouts from bystanders who took this as a real kidnapping only added to the fun. A recent promotion was celebrated with a public knighting, including an official proclamation, a sword salute, a big pile of fake money as a tribute from the king, and toy gardening tools to help to dig out of messes and to cover over complaints.

There are special toy

sales

shelves in Art's office for customers and employees to enjoy. He leaves an Etch-a-Sketch on the meeting table just to see how long people can avoid the temptation. He uses the "Silly Slammer" to deliver special messages to his agents. Art's approach to fun at work is spontaneous, creative, and inexpensive. It's an attitude that permeates the way the company operates, as well as the people who work there. It has helped to build a leading branch office as well as a stable workforce.

fun

EVENTS

GONE FUNNIN'!
BE BACK SOON

EVENTS

GONE FUNNIN'! BE BACK SOON

Fun special events are like the icing on the cake. When your organization has graduated from being a ho-hum company to a | dynamic | creative, responsive, | fun | institution, you are ready for a big event.

Fun | events | differ from the normal fun activity. I talk often about starting small, and beginning with yourself. A fun event is going BIG, and is going to include everybody, now. It is the golf outing (or golf *in*-ing), it's the company trip to the theater, it's the company-wide plane trip to Bermuda for an afternoon beach party. Fun events are bigger than life, they **are** the sort of off-the-wall behavior that is like a breath of fresh air to the staleness of corporate life. Fun events are energizers, they are **memorable** —they are the rewards that everyone has worked so hard for.

Fun events can be time-consuming to plan, and they can be expensive. But, for once a year, or once a quarter, when your organization needs a spontaneous injection of life, or a gigantic stress-relieving blowout, then the fun event is for you.

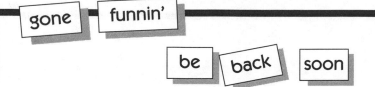

E xecutives at Home Depot decided they needed an event to help their managers realize the special significance of working for the Home Depot team and to share with them the Home Depot vision for the future. To make the impact they were looking for, they flew 4300 managers and other key employees to Atlanta for a pep rally in the Georgia Dome. At the reception, employees walked through a tunnel of cheering fans that led them to games and food on the Georgia Dome field. Included in the Home Depot invasion of Atlanta was a night at the Atlanta Civic Center, highlighted by a customized cabaret of skits and songs about being a Home Depot manager. The night concluded with a private concert put on by Glenn Frey and Joe Walsh of the late rock band, the Eagles. According to Rob Hallam, vice president of internal communications for Home Depot, "What people take back from these meetings is so important, . . . sharing the direction of the company and getting them to recharge their batteries." (*Continental*, "Executive Edge," June 2000)

fun

any companies are using theme-oriented parties or whole days to have a little fun at work. Leave it to someone at Southwest Airlines to put a new twist on the fun. Brad Newcomb, the midwest regional marketing director, thinks that even fun can be competitive. Instead of having a single theme for a company function, try having each department come up with their own theme. Prizes can be awarded to the department that best sticks to their theme. Brad points out that "a lot of camaraderie stems from this rivalry." (**Selling Power**, March 2000, "Fun Sells," Julie Sturgeon) Last year's theme contest found Brad playing Austin Powers of *The Spy Who Shagged Me*. Yeah, Baby!

▼ ▼ ▼

ometimes work-related fun events happen on their own. Spontaneity can be the key to making fun work. Gail Howerton told of her adventures working in outdoor recreation. She

events

challenged rival departments to paintball shootouts in the woods. When she planned kayaking and camping trips to train the staff on equipment and river rescue, she invited families along to build camaraderie. From what I understand, the outdoor training has been a splashing success!

▼　　▼　　▼

At Sprint's Dallas office they celebrated National Fun at Work Day (April 1, of course) by having a company-wide photo safari. Sprint split its 3000 employees into two groups and instructed them to act out 20 song titles and take photographic proof. Sprint employees jumped into the company fountain to act out "Splish Splash" while others draped their bodies over a metal railing to act out "London Bridge Is Falling Down." Donna Berry, manager of

fun

marketing programs for Sprint Business Creative Marketing Center, told *Incentive* magazine: "Since the introduction of such programs, Sprint has found increases in morale, productivity, and retention. We try to create an environment that's fun, where they can enjoy coming to work."

▼   ▼   ▼

If you look at people who are straining to be individual in a cubicle jungle, toys are one way people do it.

Chris Byrne, *Playthings MarketWatch*

▼   ▼   ▼

irst Ohio Mortgage Corporation has put a fun twist on an old office tradition. Many companies have a Secret Santa gift exchange around the holidays, but First Ohio has made the gift exchange an ornament exchange, where the recipients are randomly selected and kept secret. The person who picked the name must buy or

events

create a unique ornament that is special to the person they picked. The ornaments are hung in the office and everyone is invited to guess which ornament goes with which person. In a large office this is a great way to learn something about your co-workers. As one employee stated, "I hardly knew the person I had to make an ornament for. I had to find out more about him and what he liked. It was an easy way to meet people you wouldn't normally interact with."

▼　　▼　　▼

Linda Vos, of the Prudential Insurance Company in Roseland, New Jersey, uses her favorite fun food as a way to spur creativity in her office. Linda has a marshmallow fight to kick off

brainstorming sessions at her continuous improvement meetings. She has established a few

ground rules since getting the idea of a marshmallow fight in *301 Ways to Have Fun at Work*:

Rule #1
She highly recommends the Jet Puff
marshmallow variety for consistent ammunition.

Rule #2
Limit marshmallow fights to 90 seconds.

Rule #3
Create invisible lines of demarcation. No
trespassing beyond these boundaries.

Rule #4
The team with the least amount of
marshmallows on their side of the room
at the end of the fight wins.

Rule #5
No licking your ammunition prior to firing.

Rule #6
No eating your ammunition in order to win.

Rule #7
HAVE FUN!

events

Michelle Davis, a human resources assistant for Microlog, makes sure all the employees are in on the fun on Candy Day. The Friday before a holiday weekend she puts a candy bar on each employee's desk with a note wishing them a fun-filled weekend.

▼   ▼   ▼

Attend the Annual International Conference on the Positive Power of Humor and Creativity. Produced by The Humor Project of Saratoga Springs, New York (518-587-8770), this annual meeting focuses on the tremendous benefits of keeping humor in your professional and personal life.

▼   ▼   ▼

I was with my family in Detroit for a few baseball games last spring. While packing all our goodies prior to one last look at Tiger Stadium, a news piece came on CNN that caught

fun

my attention. Since I couldn't sit down and start writing, here are the sketchy details of one of the most spectacular events I have heard of. A New England–based furniture company decided to reward their employees with a beach party in celebration of a successful year. I have heard of many companies hosting a beach party but this company went a little further. They had the

entire company meet at Logan International Airport early one weekday morning. They then loaded up a chartered DC-10 airplane and jetted off to Bermuda. Awaiting them there were shuttles to a private beach where they barbecued, danced to a live reggae band, and frolicked in the surf and sand all day long. As the day wound down everyone was shuttled back to the airport and flown back to Boston. That was one over-the-top beach party.

A survey of 286 employers conducted by the consulting firm of William M. Mercer, Inc., revealed that only 8% incorporated fun into their work. Only 4% had ever hired a humor or fun consultant.

Entrepreneur magazine, March 2000

▼　　▼　　▼

H eather Tull, CEO of the Small Business Development Company, in Port of Spain, Trinidad, is a real fun fanatic. In the past Heather has successfully added many fun activities to her training. She recently created a fun event that she used at a company meeting. Heather broke her company up into four teams. All mixed up into a heap were four jigsaw puzzles, the 100-piece Mickey Mouse children's type puzzles. The boxes with the picture of the puzzle were clear on the other side of the room. In order to retrieve the box a team member had to go through an obstacle course blindfolded. The blindfolded person was guided by another member of his team, who was not allowed to touch him, but only guide him by the sound of his voice. The obstacle course involved doing some turns with a hula hoop, eating a small pizza, and crawling over and under a table while blindfolded. While that was going on the rest of the team had nothing better to do than to start sorting puzzle pieces. The winning team got tickets to the theater and everyone else got chocolates. "Everyone had a really great time and said that it was the best meeting we ever had. They always say that," recalled Heather.

▼   ▼   ▼

Sarah Morgan, director of clinical nutrition and dietetics at the University of Alabama at Birmingham, admits that it is difficult to keep up with fun events under a declining state budget. She has found a couple of great companies that stock inexpensive resources that can be used to spice up the fun at work.

events

Oriental Trading Company, Inc.
www.oriental.com ▼ 800-228-2269
American Science & Surplus
www.sciplus.com ▼ 847-982-0870
**Both companies have a wide selection of fun and
weird stuff, like talking door mats, stovepipe hats,
and decorations for all the holidays.**

▼　　▼　　▼

The Philippine Women's University likes to
maintain the teamwork and camaraderie of
university employees by hosting the Annual
Intercolor Fungames. The purpose of the annual
activity is to maintain a sense of unity among the
many employees who work at the university.
Everyone is included—administrators, faculty,
maintenance people, even security personnel.
Employees are intermingled in teams identified
by colors of the rainbow. Throughout the day,
participants are asked to take part in many silly
games and activities, giving everyone on the team
a chance to interact and come up with new and
unusual strategies to win the games. It is a

fun

unique opportunity for individuals who would normally have no daily interaction to learn and share experiences with each other. The feedback has been overwhelmingly positive.

▼   ▼   ▼

Fun's precipitous, serendipitous,
That's the part that is sweet,
Because the wonderful thing about fun is
It kicks you right in the seat.
Big, the Musical, **lyrics by Richard Maltby**

▼   ▼   ▼

When you need to put on a memorable fun event, you can call on people like Sharon Fisher, president of Memories Unlimited in Orlando, Florida. Many of her clients are passing on the typical trip to a conference hotel for something more special. Sharon explains: "It's no longer enough just to put on a generic meeting

events

and tell people to show up for two or three days of seminars. In order to keep people's attention you've got to engage them. . ." (*Continental*, "Executive Edge," July 2000). What Sharon recommends is that you "play with a purpose." For example, at a recent meeting planned for Roxane Laboratories of Columbus, Ohio, she arranged for 120 salespeople to go Key West, Florida, for training. The training consisted of breaking the group into five teams that rotated through five different training games based on television game shows like the *$25,000 Pyramid*. (Doesn't seem like a lot of money anymore, does it?) The questions were derived from information regarding Roxane's products and services. The winning team was awarded prizes. The meeting help build product knowledge and a sense of camaraderie, and it was a lot of fun. I think, to get with the times, the next game-show model should be *Who Wants to Be a Millionaire*.

DAVE'S TOP TEN REASONS TO
SHUT DOWN
THE OFFICE FOR THE AFTERNOON

**Afternoon baseball game
(especially if it's the Indians!)**

Video trivia at the local pub

Miniature golf

Go-kart racing

Frisbee golf in the park

Trip to an amusement park

Laser tag

Work on Habitat for Humanity house

Kickball game (indoor or outdoor)

Cruise on a boat

BONUS   BONUS   BONUS

Whirlyball game

**25-Cent Buffalo Wing Day!
(Goes great with
reasons 1 and 2)**

It may not seem like a wilderness adventure, but it had similar benefits when Estee Lauder sent its entire sales promotion department from the their offices in the concrete jungle on Fifth Avenue to the Central Park Conservatory's Professional Development Program. The event was a daylong series of activities designed to facilitate team-building and leadership skills on the park grounds. Shirley McGill thought it was great. "Just getting out of the office can stimulate a sluggish work force. You need to be outdoors. When you spend all your time in your office, at your workstation, you forget how to learn." (*LA Times*, 9/14/97, Eileen Glanton)

After playing several games on the pavement above the park conservatory garden, they tested their new skills by simulating a product development meeting. "I think we saw each other without our titles," said Cori LeVine, a director in the sales department. "It helped break down some of the barriers that might be there when we're in a business mode."

fun

166

$\mathcal{G}$ ail Howerton, CEO (chief *energizing* officer) of Funcilitators, a Massachusetts training and consulting company, has several ideas on how to keep the workplace lively:

▼ Hour flowers. Send flowers to a person with a note, "Enjoy these for an hour and then send them to someone else who may need them.

▼ Make a treasure map from a magazine. Cut out pictures of things you like or pictures that will inspire you to achieve a goal. Hang them on your wall to gaze at while taking a mental health break, daydreaming, or when you're on hold.

▼ Celebrate Secretaries Day with wacky office games like Rat Race Steeplechase or Admin-Antics. Activities include office chair races, flipping computer discs into a trash can like playing cards, or running an obstacle course with a full cup of coffee.

▼ Send hemorrhoid-o-grams to someone who's being a pain in the rear.

If you need an event that will shake up the thinking in your company, you may want to try what the Fluor Corporation did at their Irvine, California offices. At a management training meeting, children from a local school were invited to help some executives develop some new ideas to improve the workplace. A separate group of adults-only were sent to work independently from the executive/children group. At day's end the mixed group of executives and children had generated more innovative ideas than the adults-only group. One of the ideas, for a Vision Room that would contain master schedules and project engineering models, was later implemented by Fluor.

▼　　▼　　▼

Turn your office into an ongoing fun event that your employees design for themselves. At Icarian Inc. in Sunnyvale, California, CEO Doug Merritt wanted to create a profitable, fun place to work. He has done just that, expanding his offices to eight cities nationwide with an unheard-of 2% turnover rate of employees. His offices are known for the health club, sports teams, wine tastings, arcade games, pets at work, and employee musical performances. But the ongoing event of Icarian Dollars is what the employees like most. Icarian Dollars are like Monopoly money, only it can be spent on real  things. Each month all employees are given $50 to improve the workplace or enhance their own lives. Icarian Dollars have been used for golf lessons, snowboarding, and whitewater rafting trips. Sometimes employees have pooled their money to buy the company wind chimes for the lobby or a company ski trip. Many employees have funded community and charity projects with their Icarian Dollars. Icarian has found that the program helps to retain quality employees. "Being able to do so many fun things make us a lot more productive," says Icarian's purchasing manager Jenny Manassau. (**San Francisco Examiner**, August 20, 2000)

events

VIRGIN
BRANDS FUN

I have the pleasure of meeting and learning about many individuals who have made fun a part of their life, not just a part of their worklife. Richard Branson, of Virgin Companies, is one of those unique individuals who not only made his own life fun but also has made fun part of his businesses for his thousands of employees. The Virgin brand has become one of the most recognizable names in the entire world. Branson has created over 200 compa-nies worldwide, employing over 25,000 people and generating over $5 billion in revenue. Richard Branson possesses a unique combination of person-al characteristics that have made him one of the most respected "fun" business lead-ers in the world. He has the ability to include others in his fun, he communicates his vision exceedingly well to his employees (and, for that mat-ter, to his competition!), he is well trusted, doing what he says he is going to do, and he is an adventurer and risk taker. Branson believes that the reason Virgin is so success-ful is its ability to give its cus-tomers in every market value for money spent, quality, inno-vation, and a sense of fun. Their customers expect extra-ordinary things from Virgin, which puts the companies in a unique position of trust and strength. Virgin looks for opportunities where they can offer something better, fresher,

fun

and more valuable than what is already available. Branson has made his business life one big fun event.

THE BUILDING BLOCKS OF FUN

On the Virgin website (www.virgin.com), you can travel with Richard throughout the world, sharing in the fun he has working with a variety of people and businesses. Branson has a singular ability to make every event fun, while mixing it with a specific business purpose. Here are some samples from the past year:

January: Richard hosts a party of 30 children from a local primary school to unveil the world's largest LEGO train, located in London's Euston

Station. The life-sized LEGO model is designed to give the public a foretaste of a new train being introduced in 2002. The train is located in the Travel Centre at Euston Station, and will be free to visitors. The LEGO model was designed to provide some fun for young travelers while educating the public about how Virgin is revolutionizing the UK rail network.

April: Richard was in Australia to help launch a new domestic Australian airline. The new airline will be named Virgin Blue, as a result of a "name the airline" competition hosted by a local radio station. Branson stated why Virgin Blue was selected: "I've heard how Australians refer to a redhead as a "bluey" and, since our planes are red, we thought it would be a bit of fun."

ROUND TRIP FUN

May: On the BBC's top-rated evening show "Whatever You

events

Want," contestants are given the chance to compete for their dreams. One show featured three children whose dream it was to name an airplane. The winner was driven on a motorcycle to London Heathrow Airport by Richard himself to see and name the plane the "Island Lady." Richard offered all three contestants and their families all-expense-paid trips to Florida.

Still May: Richard flies to Delhi to announce the launch of the first direct flight from London to Delhi. To make his arrival appropriate (and fun) he showed up in traditional Indian dress, complete with turban and elephant. Even the Boeing 747 was decorated with an enormous flower garland.

June: Found Richard hosting the kickoff to a new business, Virgin Wines,

at the Whitechapel Art Gallery in London. According to Branson, "We set up Virgin Wines because I love wine, but don't know much about it. What I really want is someone who can tell me "If you like this, you'll love that." And most of all someone who doesn't leave me feeling like I am sitting in front of the bank manager."

IT'S THE FUN, NOT THE MONEY

Richard has the benefit of being one of the wealthiest men in the world, and critics may say that he can afford to do the exotic and elaborate fun promotions and events that Virgin creates. But, considering that he only got his start in the seventies as a small mail-order record company, I would say a lot of his success is due to his ability to make fun events out of every aspect of his business. The side benefit is that he gets money too!

THE TWELVE-STEP METHOD TO FUN

A QUICK REVIEW FOR THE FUN-IMPAIRED WORKPLACE

When Leslie Yerkes and I came up with the 12-Step Method to Fun to give individuals and companies an easy method for developing a fun workplace, we thought that by concentrating on one step per month for a year you could turn yourself and your organization into fun fanatics. Over the last few years I have found that a lot of people want to move fast when starting a fun initiative—and who can blame them? Included in this review of the 12 Steps I have added my recommendations on a Fast Start for Fun program. That I have separated some of the steps by no means diminishes the importance of the rest of the steps. I believe that, in order to sustain a fun workplace, all twelve steps need to be addressed. But, in discussions with many people, I found a recurring interest in starting fast. They had a desire to hone the 12 Steps into something they can do this week. I guess this is why *Reader's Digest* has been popular for so many years.

I selected four steps that are easy to implement and correspond with Dave's Hierarchy of Fun. I feel that these steps will help most organizations gain a firm foundation on which to build their fun workplace.

steps

1

START WITH YOURSELF

What are you waiting for? Don't wait for someone else to start the fun. Start small and build. Be clever. Having fun can be as simple as changing your title. Instead of human resources manager, how about "corporate cheerleader"? Try "goddess of fire" to replace fire prevention coordinator, or "creative paradox," which Gordon MacKenzie used at Hallmark Cards.

2

INSPIRE FUN IN OTHERS

Fun is contagious. Once you get it started, you can be an inspiration to others to take charge of the fun in their lives.

fun

3

CREATE AN ENVIRONMENT THAT ENCOURAGES FUN

If you have yourself and your co-workers thinking fun, it is time to make sure your work environment helps fun flourish. The proper environment can take fun from just an attitude to part of your culture—"the way we do things around here."

Many companies have found that a break room can be more than a table with a coffeepot. Some companies, like the cable TV Cartoon Network, have found that a brightly colored room filled with beanbag chairs is a more appropriate way to keep staffers sharp and stress-free. Many companies use the break room/ lunchroom as "fun central," using the space to play with stress-relieving toys (Koosh balls are great) or, to post their favorite comic strips and humorous pictures of co-workers.

steps

4

CELEBRATE THE BENEFITS OF FUN

Remember to acknowledge that fun helps you accomplish great things. If a Hawaiian Beach Party causes you to set a sales record, celebrate by creating a fun workplace and acknowledge that you and your co-workers were able to move mountains.

5

ELIMINATE BOUNDARIES AND OBSTACLES THAT INHIBIT FUN.

Communicate with those who are putting up roadblocks. Most obstacles to a fun workplace are due to poor communication and therefore a lack of trust from authority figures. In order to build trust, start small and build on

FAST START

fun

your successes. It could be as easy as agreeing to have an ice-cream social if a productivity target is met. Remember to communicate the objectives for having fun and the resultant fun reward clearly. Build trust, and you eliminate boundaries and obstacles.

LOOK FOR THE HUMOR IN YOUR SITUATION

Always be ready to laugh, especially at yourself. It takes a good sense of humor to deal with the plethora of absurdities that crop up at work.

(Sometimes things happen that are not suited to a family publication like this.) The organizations that best deal with adversity are the ones who find humor in the situation.

Maria Raper, of La Quinta Hotels, found that part of the training for new hires at the corporate office was to spend time at one of the inns working every shift and position, including cleaning the toilets. Upon completion of the training, each employee received a trophy with a toilet on top, a reward which Maria still proudly displays.

7

FOLLOW YOUR INTUITION. BE SPONTANEOUS

As the Nike ads say, DO IT NOW. If you wait or postpone your fun, you will find that, after a short 12 months, you have had a great year of intentions. Time flies, and we are all easily distracted. I am told this malady is called FTI, or failure to implement. So, if suddenly the mood takes you to play a round of inner-office Frisbee golf, then do it.

fun

DON'T POSTPONE YOUR FUN

Schedules are great for keeping order in a hectic life. Remember though, if you always schedule fun to take place tomorrow, you will never have fun.

MAKE FUN INCLUSIVE

FAST START

There is nothing less fun than being excluded from a little office humor or a group activity. Fun can only occur in a workplace that gives everyone the opportunity to participate in games, events, and even an office joke. If you find yourself reading an e-mail joke that you can't

share with everyone without being embarrassed, then that joke that should go straight to the trash bin. Fun is for everyone.

Remember how Michele Davis, a human resources assistant for Microlog, includes all the employees in the fun on Candy Day. The Friday before a holiday weekend she puts a candy bar on each employee's desk with a note wishing them a fun-filled weekend (my favorite fun candy bars are Payday and $100,000 Bar).

10

SMILE, AND LAUGH A LOT

The best fun tools you can use are your beautiful smile and a hearty belly laugh. I dare anyone to keep from joining the fun with these most potent fun weapons.

fun

11

BECOME KNOWN AS FUN-LOVING

Become the self-actualized fun person. At the top of Dave's Hierarchy of Fun is Identity. Make it a part of your identity to become known as a real fun person to be around.

12

PUT FUN INTO ACTION

FAST START

Take an idea a day and put it into action. It doesn't need to be overwhelming or special (or, it can be), but make sure you put your ideas into action daily. You have a blank canvas on which you paint the reflection of your life. Make it bold and beautiful and fun. But, most of all, make sure the canvas is full to the edges.

steps

FAST START FOR
FUN REVIEW

Start with yourself.

Eliminate boundaries and obstacles that inhibit fun.

Make fun inclusive.

Put fun into action.

SUGGESTED READINGS

Adams, Scott. *The Dilbert Future: Thriving on Stupidity in the 21st Century.* New York: HarperCollins, 1997.

Carlaw, Peggy, and Kathleen Deming. *Big Book of Sales Games.* New York: McGraw-Hill, 1999.

Carlaw, Peggy, and Kathleen Deming. *Big Book of Customer Service Training Games.* New York: McGraw-Hill, 1998.

Deems, Richard S. *Hiring: How to Find and Keep the Best People.* Franklin Lakes, NJ: Career Press, 1998.

Davis, Alan. *The Fun Also Rises: The Most Fun Places to Be at the Right Time.* San Francisco: Greenline Publications, 1998.

Epstein, Robert. *Big Book of Stress Relief Games.* New York: McGraw-Hill, 2000.

Gessel, Izzy. *Playing Along: 37 Group Learning Activities Borrowed from Improvisational Theater.* Duluth, MN: Whole Person Press, 1997.

Greenwich, Carolyn. *Fun Factor: Games, Sales Contests, and Activities That Make Work Fun.* New York: McGraw-Hill, 1997.

Hemsath, Dave, and Leslie Yerkes. *301 Ways to Have Fun at Work.* San Francisco: Berrett-Koehler, 1997.

Herman, Roger E. *Keeping Good People: Strategies for Solving the #1 Problem Facing Business Today.* Winchester, VA: Oakhill Press, 1998.

Hoffman, Ellen. *Rock the Casbah: Complete Instructions for Twelve Unforgettable, Fabulous Adult Parties.* New York: Dell, 1996.

Kaye, Beverly, and Sharon Jordan-Evans. *Love 'Em or Lose 'Em: Getting Good People to Stay.* San Francisco: Berrett-Koehler, 1999.

Leigh, Elyssebeth, and Jeff Kinder. *Learning Through Fun and Games.* New York: McGraw-Hill, 2000.

MacKenzie, Gordon. *Orbiting the Giant Hairball: A Corporate Fool's Guide to Surviving with Grace*. Shawnee Mission, KS: OpusPocus, 1996.

Mornell MD, Pierre, and Kit Hinrichs. *Games Companies Play: A Job-Hunter's Guide to Playing Smart.* Berkeley, CA: Ten Speed Press, 2000.

Newstrom, John, and Edward Scannell. *Big Book of Business Games*. New York: McGraw-Hill, 1995.

Newstrom, John, and Edward Scannell. *Big Book of Presentation Games.* New York: McGraw-Hill, 1997.

Newstrom, John, and Edward Scannell. *Big Book of Team Building Games.* New York: McGraw-Hill, 1998.

Reynolds, Larry. *Trust Effect: Creating the High Trust, High Performance Organization.* London: Nicholas Brealey, 1997.

Shaw, Robert B. *Trust in the Balance: Building Successful Organizations on Results, Integrity, and Concern.* San Francisco: Jossey-Bass, 1997.

Tamblyn, Doni. *Big Book of Humorous Training Games.* New York: McGraw-Hill, 2000.

Terr MD, Lenore. *Beyond Love and Work: Why Adults Need to Play.* New York: Touchstone, 2000.

Warner, Penny. *Big Book of Party and Holiday Fun.* Minnetonka, MN: Meadowbrook, 2000.

Weinstein, Matt. *Managing to Have Fun.* New York: Fireside, 1997.

Yerkes, Leslie. *Fun Works*. San Francisco: Berrett-Koehler, 2001.

HIRING & RETENTION

Page 19
Tim Puet, "High-tech firm keeps employees with lure of free housework." *Cleveland Plain Dealer*, 9/5/99.

Page 25
Continental, "Executive edge." September 1999.

Page 25
Dayton Fandray, "Recruiting online." *Continental*, September 1999.

Page 26
Feliciano Garcia and Karen Vella-Zarb. "The 100 Best Companies to Work For." *Fortune*, 1/10/00.

Page 31
Gillian Flynn, "Face it: Jobs can use a few laughs." *San Francisco Examiner*, 12/28/97.

Page 33
Sabrina Jones, "Firms put fun in the workplace." *Raleigh News & Observer*, October 1999.

CORPORATE CULTURE

Page 49
Scripps Howard New Service, "Mixing work and fun often the best recipe." *Colorado Springs Gazette*, 10/25/99.

Page 49
Tony Mosely, "Casting for customer service." *Customer Service Management*, September/October 1999.

Page 56
Suzanne Alexander, "Where you lose to win." *Cleveland Plain Dealer*, 12/21/98.

Page 60
Lynne Thompson, "Workspace: Playspace." *Cleveland Style*, August 1998.

LEADERSHIP

Page 76
Kenneth Hein, "Funny Business." *Incentive,* April 1998.

Page 77-80
Tony Mosely, "Fun and Profit at Southwest Airlines." *Customer Service Management*, May/June 1999.

Page 81
Ruby Bailey, "Funny business." *Detroit Free Press*, 5/22/99.

Page 94
Gillian Flynn, "Face it: Jobs can use a few laughs." *San Francisco Examiner*, 12/28/97.

CUSTOMER SERVICE

Page 115
Bulletin Board, *Disney* magazine, Fall 2000.

Page 118
"Fun and games keep them smiling at NovaCare. North Coast '99." *Cleveland Plain Dealer*, 9/24/00.

SALES AND MARKETING

Page 130
Erika Rasmussen, "A funny thing happened on the way to work." *Sales & Marketing Management*, March 1999.

Page 133
Rodd Aubrey, "Dousing stress with a squirt gun." *Cleveland Plain Dealer*, 7/4/98

Page 135
Joan Patterson, "Experts agree levity brings more than laughs to stressful workplace." *Las Vegas Review-Journal*, 2/23/99.

Page 136
Kenneth Hein, "Funny business." *Incentive,* April 1998.

Page 136
Daniel Roth, "My job at the container store." *Fortune,* 1/17/00.

Page 145
Refina Brett, "Life's ducky with brokerage." *Cleveland Plain Dealer*, 10/24/00.

EVENTS

Page 155
Kenneth Hein, "Funny business." *Incentive*, April 1998.

Page 163
Chris Warren, "Memorable meetings." *Continental*, July 2000.

Page 166
Eileen Glanton, "Corporate America takes a playful approach to workplace cooperation." *Los Angeles Times*, 9/14/97.

Page 169
Carol Kleiman, "Monopoly money makes work a party—as long as it lasts." *San Francisco Examiner,* 8/20/00.

INDEX

COMPANIES FEATURED

ABOUT THE AUTHOR

D ave Hemsath is co-owner and founder of BreakPoint Books and More (formerly Business Outreach Books) in Rocky River, Ohio. BreakPoint is the nation's largest supplier of onsite bookstores for conferences and conventions. He has also created Dave's Idea Company (as his book-writing persona) to help organizations find the fun in work. Dave speaks to professionals on the benefits of a fun workplace and helps to energize companies and organizations to perform their best.

Dave is known for his outrageous behavior at work. Several of the ideas from this book and his previous writing are used at his office. Dave's co-workers know they are just guinea pigs for some of the ideas (for example, a bamboo speaking staff), but they amuse him and play along. If he dresses to impress, he will be in a Hawaiian shirt and a do rag. Some of his favorite ideas are shutting down the office for an afternoon of watching the Indians play baseball, 25-cent wing day at BW3's, and trying goofy props to liven up office staff meetings.

For the last several years, Dave has had the pleasure of addressing many organizations and conferences regarding the benefits of a fun workplace. His sessions are known for the interaction between Dave and the audience, and for being LOUD. Everyone has a lot of fun. The program examines the benefits of fun at work and provides practical examples of ways to incorporate new attitudes and new approaches into the life of any business. The unique and exciting how-tos are designed to enliven the work environment, meetings, team activities, customer service, hiring, sales and marketing, internal and external communications, and recognition programs.

Dave was graduated from The Ohio State University with degrees in marketing and production management. His many years of sales and marketing experience have brought him the opportunity to teach and speak to several local high schools and colleges. Dave has published many articles in national trade publications and newspapers, and he is continuing to gather material for future book projects.

Dave lives in Strongsville, Ohio, with his wife Gayle and their three boys Michael (call me Mike!), Derek, and Scott. When not traveling, Dave prefers to spend his time with his boys, coaching baseball (Go Storm!), watching all the boys' sporting events, attending Derek's plays, and playing with Scott. Dave believes that in a perfect world the Indians would win a World Series.

Dave Hemsath can be reached at hemsath@msn.com, or at:

BreakPoint Books and More
19135 Hilliard Blvd.
Rocky River, OH 44116
(440) 895-6000